Nuclear Multilateralism and Iran

T0384915

Drawing on the author's personal experience, this book presents an insider's chronology and policy analysis of the EU's role in the nuclear negotiations with Iran.

The European Union strives to be a global player, a "soft power" leader that can influence international politics and state behavior. Yet critics argue that the EU's Common Foreign and Security Policy (CFSP) remains largely ineffective and incoherent. The EU's early and continuous involvement in the effort to dissuade Iran from developing nuclear weapons can be viewed as a test case for the EU as a global actor. As Chair of the European Parliament's delegation for relations with Iran, Tarja Cronberg had a ringside seat in the negotiations to prevent Iran from developing nuclear weapons. Drawing on her experiences leading a parliamentary delegation to Iran and interviews with officials, legislators and opposition leaders in nearly every country participating in the negotiations, as well as reports by the International Atomic Energy Agency, parliaments and independent experts, the author illustrates an insider's strategic understanding of the negotiations. Intersecting history, politics, economics, culture and the broader security context, this book not only delivers a unique analysis of this historic deal and the twelve-year multilateral pursuit of it, but draws from it pertinent lessons for European policy makers for the future.

This book will be of much interest to students of nuclear proliferation, EU policy, diplomacy and international relations in general.

Tarja Cronberg is a Distinguished Associate Fellow with the European Security Programme at SIPRI, Sweden, and a member of the Board of the European Leadership Network. She is a former member of the European Parliament where she chaired the delegation for relations with Iran.

Nuclear Multilateralism and Iran

Inside EU Negotiations

Tarja Cronberg

Routledge
Taylor & Francis Group

LONDON AND NEW YORK

First published 2017
by Routledge

2 Park Square, Milton Park, Abingdon, Oxfordshire OX14 4RN
52 Vanderbilt Avenue, New York, NY 10017

Routledge is an imprint of the Taylor & Francis Group, an informa business

First issued in paperback 2020

British Library Cataloguing-in-Publication Data
A catalogue record for this book is available from the British Library

Library of Congress Cataloging-in-Publication Data
Names: Cronberg, Tarja, author.
Title: Nuclear multilateralism and Iran : inside EU negotiations / Tarja Cronberg.
Description: Abingdon, Oxon ; New York, NY : Routledge, 2017. | Includes bibliographical
references and index.
Identifiers: LCCN 2016048452| ISBN 9781138283855 (hardback) |
ISBN 9781315269962 (ebook)
Subjects: LCSH: Nuclear nonproliferation—Government policy—European Union countries.
| Nuclear weapons—Iran. | Common Foreign and Security Policy. | European Union
countries—Foreign relations—Iran. | Iran—Foreign relations—European Union countries.
Classification: LCC JZ5675 .C76 2017 | DDC 327.1/7470955—dc23LC record available at
https://lccn.loc.gov/2016048452

ISBN: 978-1-138-28385-5 (hbk)
ISBN: 978-0-367-60741-8 (pbk)

Typeset in Times New Roman
by diacriTech, Chennai

Contents

Preface

As a researcher at the Finnish Institute of International Affairs, I had written a report on nuclear weapons and the Nuclear Non-Proliferation Treaty as background for the 2010 NPT Review Conference. Then, in June 2011, I became a Member of the European Parliament (MEP). A few months later, I was elected Chair of the Parliament´s delegation for relations with Iran. Now a politician, my interest in nuclear weapons and the role of international treaties assumed a new perspective and urgency. The Iran nuclear issue was at the frontlines of these issues, with the possibility of sanctions up for debate within the EU.

The Parliament had, of course, no role in the actual negotiations. These were carried out by a team directly under EU High Representative Catherine Ashton. The Lisbon Treaty requires that EU foreign and security policy is to be carried out in cooperation with the Parliament. Consequently, we, members of the foreign affairs committee, received regular briefings on the status of the negotiations and related EU policies. My role as Chair of the delegation for relations with Iran was, according to the mandate for delegations, to maintain relations with Iran and inform the parliament.

The Iran delegation arranged hearings and invited experts to speak at our meetings. We had regular contacts with think tanks and other organizations, especially on human rights, working on Iran. The delegation´s main contact with Iran was the Iranian Embassy in Brussels. Although we were supposed to travel to Iran for interparliamentary dialogues, this turned out to be difficult. In 2011, as the delegation was about to leave, our visas were delayed by the embassy. Just a few days prior, MEK, an Iranian opposition group, had staged an event in the European Parliament.

In 2012, our trip was to take place immediately after the European Parliament had awarded the Sakharov Prize for Freedom of Thought to two Iranians: the human rights lawyer Nasrin Soutudeh and the film instructor Janar Panahi. Our visit was widely publicized and we got thousands of letters from Iranian opposition groups others telling us not go. The US

Senate sent a letter to President of the Parliament Martin Schulz asking the delegation to reconsider its visit and that the President does what he can to indefinitely postpone this ill-advised trip at this sensitive time.

The president was supportive of the trip, but the EP presidium decided, the day before we were to leave, that we had to receive permission to meet the Sakharov Prize winners in prison, as a precondition for the trip. The EP sent this message to the Iranian embassy late on a Friday night. The ambassador called me the next day, a few hours before the delegation members were to leave for Iran, that it had not been able to arrange the visit: the time was limited and he had not been able to get in touch with officials in Iran late Friday night as their weekend had started and it was prayer time. I canceled the trip and we unpacked our suitcases.

In December 2013, the delegation finally made it to Tehran, half a year after the surprise election of the moderate President Hassan Rouhani and a couple of weeks after the interim Joint Plan of Action was agreed on November 24. We met with the "official" Iran: parliamentarians, the foreign minister, former President Ali Akbar Hashemi Rafsanjani and representatives of the newly elected president´s cabinet. We also met with civil society: environmental, feminist and citizen groups. We managed to arrange a meeting with both Sakharov Prize winners, now under house arrest. We had an interesting dialogue with the ambassadors of the EU member states in Tehran and the representatives of different branches of UN institutions.

These years in the EP and as chair of the Iran delegation form the source of my knowledge on Iran. During that time, the EP approved of a number of resolutions, not only on Iran but also on the Middle East weapons-of-mass-destruction-free zone. During the plenary debates, it was obvious that the EP was divided between those wanting to isolate Iran and those who saw dialogue as the way forward.

In 2014, while still in the parliament, together with HR Catherine Ashton, I received the Iranian Wet Gunpowder Award. The prize, given by the Basij commander each year in close cooperation with the Islamic Revolutionary Guards Corps, is given to someone who is against the Islamic Revolution and who against their own wishes, performs a service to the revolution. The year before it had gone to Michelle Obama.

In addition to my work within the EU system in 2011-14, I had, as Chair of the Iran delegation, a chance to talk about Iran. I often visited the United States to attend seminars at US think tanks such as the Center for Strategic and International Studies, the Carnegie Endowment for International Peace, the Arms Control Association, and the National Iran-American Council. When the 2012 trip to Iran was canceled, I traveled to Turkey to talk with Iranian professors working in Istanbul and with the Turkish Foreign Ministry in Ankara. On a visit to India in 2013, I had the chance to discuss EU sanctions policy with Indian experts. In 2015, during the final negotiations, I interviewed senior European External Action Service and national officials as well as Brussels-based think tanks. I spent a month in Washington, DC, at the Woodrow Wilson International Center for Scholars interviewing former negotiators, congressmen, their advisors and think-tank experts. From this wide range of consultations, interviews, discussions, research, analysis and experience, the following book has emerged. At the time of this writing, in January 2017, the implementation of the Iran deal has its one year anniversary. Althought there are different interpretations of the conditions, the first year has been successful blocking Iranian pathways to nuclear weapons. As the US administration changes in 2017, the Iran deal has gained new actuality. Its provisions will be questioned and debated on both sides. My hope is that this book will provide the necessary background for these debates.

Copenhagen.
Tarja Cronberg

Acknowledgments

I am very grateful to President Martti Ahtisaari, whose initial support made this book possible. I want to thank Professor Morten Kelstrup, Department of Political Science, University of Copenhagen for inspiring dialogues on EU foreign policy and Director Tariq Rauf, SIPRI for his insights in the non-proliferation regime and the IAEA. Special thanks go to Morag Donaldson, the administrator of the Secretariat of the Delegation for Relations with Iran, European Parliament. My stay at the Woodrow Wilson International Centre for Scholars in February-March 2015 was not only a platform for interviews in the US but also for discussions with two knowledgeable persons on Iran: Directors Robert Litwak (security studies) and Haleh Esfandiari (Middle East). The Finnish Institute in Rome enabled creative concentration in October 2014 and November 2015. Persons interviewed and my collegues at the European Parliament and at SIPRI have all contributed with experience and knowledge, the interpretation of which is my sole responsibility. My research assistant Nora Westerlund and editors Rhianna Tyson Kreger and Daniel Horner have transformed thoughts and texts into a readable form. The editing was supported by the Leo Mechelin foundation in Finland.

Abbreviations

CFSP	Common Foreign and Security Policy
E3	Three EU member states: France, Germany and the UK
E3+3	European Union/France, Germany, UK + China, Russia and the US
EEAS	European External Action Service
EP	European Parliament
ESDP	European Security and Defence Policy
EU	European Union
EU/E3+3	European Union/France, Germany and the UK and China, Russia and the US
HEU	High Enriched Uranium, Weapons Grade (90% U-235)
IAEA	International Atomic Energy Agency
IRGC	Islamic Revolutionary Guard Corps
LEU	Low Enriched Uranium, Reactor Grade (3–5% U-235)
MEK	Iranian Opposition Group Mojahedin-e-Khalq
NAM	Non-Aligned Movement
NNWS	Non-Nuclear Weapon States
NPT	Nuclear Non-Proliferation Treaty
NSG	Nuclear Suppliers' Group
NWS	Nuclear Weapon States
PMD	Possible Military Dimension
P5+1	UN Security Council Members (China, France, Russia, UK and US) + Germany
TRR	Teheran Research Reactor
UN	United Nations
UNGA	United Nations General Assembly
UNMOVIC	United Nations Monitoring, Verification and Inspection Commission
UNSC	United Nations Security Council
UNSCOM	United Nations Special Commission (Mandated to Conduct Inspections in Iraq)

Introduction

The image of the European Union is no longer one of a model for the world but one of crises: the euro crisis, the refugee crisis and now Brexit. These crises have dominated the news and given the impression of a union without vision and unable to act together. In the shadows of these crises, the EU has been instrumental in making the world a safer place and in preventing a war. Not a small achievement for a Union the foundations of which are built on peace.

Nuclear weapons are the greatest threat to mankind. William Perry, a former US secretary of defense, asserts in his book "My Journey at the Nuclear Brink" that the risk for a nuclear catastrophe is today greater than it was during the Cold War. The European Union, together with its international partners, has averted one of the risks through diplomacy. The Iran deal, the Joint Comprehensive Plan of Action (JCPOA), blocks Iran's paths to nuclear weapons and through restrictions on its nuclear program, makes sure that the nuclear program is entirely peaceful.

The deal was a result of a European initiative, in 2003, to initiate diplomatic discussions with Iran on the nuclear threat. It took twelve years of negotiations, two American presidents and three Iranian presidents before the final deal was concluded. Why? Because the Iranians had hidden some activities. Because hostile relations between Iran and the US have prevailed since the Islamic Revolution of 1979. Because of the ambiguity of the international treaty governing nuclear disarmament and non-proliferation.

Iran has been a party to this treaty, the Nuclear Non-Proliferation Treaty, since its early years. According to the treaty all countries have the right to peaceful uses of nuclear technology, such as nuclear power or medical treatments. The conflict has been whether there is a right for a state to control its fuel cycle, the cycle leading from a uranium mine to the fuel rods of a power plant. This cycle includes a sensitive part, the enrichment of uranium, where a diversion to military uses may take place. Iran has maintained that it has the right to enrich uranium. The Americans have claimed there is no such right. The Europeans have been caught in the middle of this stride.

The European Union wants to be a global actor and Iran's nuclear program became a demonstration of the possibility. In the process the EU has tested both "carrots," such as trade, and "sticks," such as sanctions. In the effort to prevent Iran from building the bomb, the EU cooperated with the most powerful actors in the world: the US, China and Russia. Failures and successes have alternated in a process leading first to an interim agreement in November 2013 and in July 2015 to a final deal. The first objective of this book is to analyze the lessons learned from this process in relation to "effective multilateralism," the vision of the EU's foreign and security policy.

Iran wants to be a regional power. Its nuclear program is a symbol of this ambition. Iran has walked a tight rope of demanding its rights all the while not always following the rules. The negotiating powers have suspected that Iran had military intentions; Iran has claimed that the program was entirely peaceful. Iran has tested the limits of the Nuclear Non-Proliferation Treaty, the NPT, thus providing critical insight into how to manage non-proliferation in the future. The second objective of this book is to explore the need to transform the non-proliferation regime given the lessons learned from the Iran nuclear issue.

To tie these two strings together, the EU's desire to be a global actor and the need to transform the nuclear non-proliferation regime, the focus of the book is on the EU as a global, non-proliferation actor. The EU has as its members both nuclear and non-nuclear weapon states and has, consequently, been seen as a weak actor in this field. The Iran negotiations tell a different story. Without the EU, the nuclear deal would not have been possible.

The book is structured in the following way:

The two first chapters introduce the context. The first chapter creates the conceptual framework for studying the EU-Iran nuclear negotiations. The experience of the EU as a global actor is reviewed and the following questions posed: What is "effective multilateralism," the vision of the EU's foreign and security policy? How is "effective multilateralism" related to non-proliferation and what is the experience of the EU as a non-proliferation actor?

The second chapter tells the story of the nuclear negotiations from 2003 to 2015, starting with persuasive engagement as three European foreign ministers decided to talk to Iran. There is no agreement, only partial success, and Iran is reported to the Security Council. Since the pressure is not enough to contain Iran, the US and the EU introduce unilateral sanctions in a dual-track policy. It is only after the Iranian presidential elections that the political will on both sides leads to a final deal.

The next two chapters deal with the negotiations, first the process then the substance. The third chapter explores the multilateral negotiations, the actors and their relations. The role of the EU turns from an autonomous negotiator to one of a coordinator of the team (China, France, Germany, Russia, the UK and the US) and finally to a facilitator of the US-Iran bilateral talks. The transatlantic link is a special focus as the US and EU policies towards Iran oscillate between isolation and dialogue, between coercion and diplomacy. Russia and China intervene as do Turkey and Brazil.

Chapter 4 deals with the substance of the negotiations. The right to uranium enrichment is the central theme complemented by the verification problems related to the potential military dimension. The International Atomic Energy Agency is the judge on the core question: Was the nuclear program peaceful or did it have a military dimension? There seems to be "good" and "bad" proliferators as countries are treated differently. The chapter concludes with answers to two questions: What did Iran want to do? What were its intentions?

The next two chapters deal with the tools the international community disposes of when pressuring a country to not to build a bomb: sanctions and military threats. The fifth chapter introduces sanctions as economic warfare to change the target country's behavior. Iran's ideological response is the "resistance" economy to cope with the economic and humanitarian consequences. Sanctions are easier to approve than to dismantle and conflicts related to the lifting of the sanctions are already burdening the implementation of the deal.

To prevent a war with Iran in the aftermath of the Iraq war was a declared goal of the EU initiative. In chapter 6 the potential attack on Iran is viewed based on previous military strikes on nuclear facilities in the Middle East. The interaction between Israel and the US in the planning phase of potential Iran strikes is analyzed as well as the EU's role in using sanctions to prevent a strike in 2011-2012. Negotiations in general, and EU sanctions in particular, did prevent a military strike. The US military option is still on the table, but expected to be used only if actual bomb-grade material is produced.

The final chapter concludes on the policy lessons learned for the nonproliferation regime. The regime fails to meet the requirements of a rule-based system, where states are treated equally. Preconditions and regime change policies prevent results. Remedies are proposed ranging from the reduction of ambiguity to the question of who should negotiate the abolition of nuclear weapon programs. The EU's strategic capacity to frame negotiations is an asset, but the autonomy of its foreign policy is hidden behind the transatlantic link. Finally, in order to become a global actor in nonproliferation the EU is presented with three non-proliferation challenges.

1   The EU in the Current Nuclear Order

The EU is, as a result of the Iran deal, a prominent actor in non-proliferation. To have coordinated a major, twelve-year diplomatic effort, with the participation of the superpowers qualifies the EU to the rank of global actors. The EU is often criticized for a lack of strategy. The Iran nuclear issue was different. Both an EU security strategy and a non-proliferation strategy were approved at the outset of the negotiations in December 2003.

This chapter introduces the focus of these strategies: the concept of effective multilateralism. Support for a rule-based international system, where laws and norms affect all states equally and where the UN is the central framework, is the core content in effective multilateralism. The Iran nuclear program is about non-proliferation, the rules and norms of which are defined in the Nuclear Non-Proliferation Treaty, the NPT. What kind of actor is the EU in relation to the NPT?

The Grand Vision: Effective Multilateralism

> We want international organizations, regimes and treaties to be effective in confronting threats to international peace and security, and must therefore be ready to act when their rules are broken.

This is the core content of the European Security Strategy as agreed upon in 2003 (Council of the European Union, 2003b). Multilateralism for the EU is the natural, inevitable approach of an actor which itself is a multilateral undertaking. What was new in 2003 was its institutionalization on the strategic level and indeed for European foreign policy writ large (Biscop, 2004). This codifies the EU commitment to international law, well-functioning international institutions and a rules-based international order, the fundamental framework of which is the United Nations Charter.

Javier Solana, the first EU High Representative for the EU's foreign policy (HR), interpreted effective multilateralism as "multilateralism with teeth," stating further that "the world needs more, not less, multilateralism [... which] must be action-oriented and capable of delivering results" (in Koops, 2011:81). In policy terms, the task of the EU is to promote the universality of treaties and effective verification of compliance with regime obligations.

As a vision of the European Security Strategy and a founding general principle for EU foreign policy, effective multilateralism was also—even foremost—a reaction to the 2003 war and subsequent occupation of Iraq. One of the senior officials involved in writing the strategy in 2003 explains:

> Effective multilateralism was an explicit critique of the US behavior in Iraq. Iraq was a case of ineffective unilateralism. In the view of the EU, at least the US should have let the IAEA finish their work with inspections and consult the UN. My preference is that there always is a legal framework.[1]

The official, quoted above, also regrets that the phrase "effective multilateralism" is often used without a clear meaning. So how do the scholars of EU foreign policy understand this concept? Sven Biscop (2005) argues for effective multilateralism as "enforceable multilateralism." Hanna Ojanen (2004) notes the importance of commonly agreed norms and institutions and the need for "preparedness to take action against such actors that break the norms and insist on being outlaws."

Kienzle (2008) presents a more critical view. According to him, to view "effective multilateralism" as a reaction to the Iraq War is over-simplistic. The concept has deeper roots in the absence of an EU strategic concept, particularly in the field of non-proliferation. "Effective multilateralism" papers over important weaknesses within the Union: its need for cohesion and identity, its need for strategic coherence, and its need for legitimacy as an international actor.

Given this vision—and its different interpretations—the questions that will be answered in the following chapters are: How was "effective multilateralism" exercised in the Iran negotiations? Was the EU a unified actor during the process? Was the EU, together with its partners, able to enforce the rules and norms in the field of non-proliferation in a fair way, and will it be able to do so in the future? This chapter defines the platform for this analysis.

Defining (Nuclear) Multilateralism

Multilateralism is the "practice of coordinating national policies in groups of three or more states through ad hoc arrangements or by means of institutions" (Keohane, 1990:731). In the nuclear field, this coordination takes place in a number of institutions such as the Nuclear Non-Proliferation Treaty (NPT) review conferences, the International Atomic Energy Agency (the IAEA), the Nuclear Supplier's Group (NSG) and regional organizations for nuclear weapon-free zones just to name a few.

There are three constitutive principles in multilateralism according to Ruggie (1993:569–574). The first is *indivisibility*, such as in collective security arrangements where an attack on one is seen as an attack on all. The second is *nondiscrimination*, which implies that all parties are treated similarly. The third is diffuse reciprocity. States do not rely on specific *quid pro quo* exchanges but on long-term balances. Diffuse reciprocity is the constitutive principle of all multilateralism:

> Crucially, according to this approach, benefits need not materialize straight away, which makes multilateral gain-expectation fundamentally different from more utilitarian expectations often found in bilateral agreements, which normally imply the instantaneous materialization of some short term gains. (Koops, 2011:69)

Effective multilateralism within international organizations is not an easy task. There are nearly 200 member states in the United Nations and over 190 parties to the NPT. Multilateralism can become dysfunctional not only due to the number of actors, but also because states "simply lack the ability to comply with their international obligations" (van Oudenaren, 2003:4). The answer to this dysfunctional multilateralism has been that powerful states take over the coordination of policy. This has been defined as "minilateralism," meaning "great power cooperation within multilateral institutions" (Kahler 1992:296–299). This cooperation can be institutionalized as in the case of the UN Security Council, but also be more ad hoc, depending on the circumstances.

This opens the door to "adhoc multilateralism": a case-by-case form of multilateralism that allows more space for the interests of the great powers and the power relations between them. The Iran negotiations were a case of ad hoc multilateralism: on the one side, the three European states (France, Germany and the UK) and three superpowers (China, Russia and the US), coordinated by the EU, negotiated with Iran on the other side. In spite of its ad hoc nature, the group was amazingly stable during the whole process, culminating in a final deal in July 2015. Furthermore, the group will continue to monitor the implementation of the deal in the coming 10–15 years.

Power relations play a critical role in multilateralism, especially in nuclear multilateralism, as the five accepted nuclear weapon states control the decisions of the Security Council. In their essay "Conceptualizing Multilateralism," Bouchard and Peterson address these power relations. They divide multilateralism into eras of "traditional" and "new" multilateralism. Traditional multilateralism covers the theory and practice from the Second World War to the late 1980s. New multilateralism emerges after the Cold War. They found real substance to the claim that the twenty-first century "new" multilateralism is more binding, rule-based and demanding than the traditional more power-oriented, which, however, still lives in many international institutions including the UN. As a result, their pragmatic definition of multilateralism introduces relativity through the parenthetical "more or less":

> Multilateralism is three or more actors engaging in voluntary and (more or less) institutionalized international cooperation governed by norms and principles, with rules that apply (more or less) equally to all. (Bouchard and Peterson, 2011:21)

The US and EU understand power relations within multilateralism differently; whereas the latter advocates for effective multilateralism, the United States prefers the concept of *assertive* multilateralism. This divide is a red thread throughout the entire Iran process. The US Ambassador to the UN, Madeleine Albright has defined "assertive multilateralism" as:

> a way for us to take a leadership role along with others.... Assertive multilateralism for me is using the new setting of the international community to bring about agendas that are good not only for the United States, but the entire world by asserting American leadership within a particular setting and realizing assertive multilateralism has a multiplier effect. (Albright, 1993)

While assertive multilateralism may be good for the world, it is for Albright closely linked to US interests. She underlines that, unless the US exercises leadership within collective bodies like the United Nations, there is a risk that multilateralism will not serve US national interests well and may even undermine them.

For the US, multilateralism is a means to an end, but for Europeans, it is an end in itself. This distinction is further elaborated by Robert Kagan, who in 2003, as a supporter of the George W. Bush administration's unilateralism, referred to the US understanding of effective multilateralism as "a distinctly US utilitarian and outcome-oriented brand of multilateralism" (Kagan, 2003:144). According to him, the European form of effective multilateralism is more formal and legalistic, and international bodies must be consulted as a prerequisite for action.

For Kagan, multilateralism is a "weapon of the weak," meaning that states that seek multilateral arrangements lack the power to impose solutions to international problems that serve their own interests. A special dimension, but a decisive one in the Iran case, is the role of the Security Council. For the Americans, support of the Security Council is "desirable but never essential" (Kagan, 2003:144). This contrasts the EU's insistence on the Security Council as the authority.

The European understanding of effective multilateralism has to be seen not only as the rules-based international system and a goal of the EU's foreign and security policy, but also as a reaction to the US unilateralism in the Iraq war. President Bush's "coalition of the willing" that bypassed Security Council authority in the run-up to the Iraq war was a direct misuse of international institutions as a "tool for convenience," according to Martin (2003:13). In relation to this, Dennis Ross has interpreted US unilateral policies as poorly conducted "multilateralism." In his conclusion he states: "the Bush administration's failing has not been its instinct for unilateralism and its disdain for multilateralism, its failing too often has been how poorly it has practiced multilateralism" (Ross, 2008:5).

Unilateralism and bilateralism are not the only counter-positions to multilateralism. Contested multilateralism, by Morse and Keohane, is a phenomenon that occurs when states and/or non-state actors either shift their focus from one existing institution to another or create an alternative multilateral institution to compete with an existing one (Morse and Keohane, 2014). The Joint Commission, an organization created by the Iran deal to monitor the implementation of the deal, will be dealt with as an example.

The Aspiration to Become a Global Actor

The EU's capacity to act outside its borders and convince other countries to change their behavior is contested. It is by no means given that the EU can be a global actor in foreign and security policy, despite the European Security Strategy's assertion that the EU, merely due to its size, is a global actor (Council of the European Union, 2003b:1). Bretherton and Vogler (1999) comprehensively analyzed the EU as a global actor in various policy fields. Their conclusion is that foreign and security policy is the field where the gap between ambition and reality is the greatest.

This is explained by the EU's long and agonizing pursuit of recognition as a legitimate foreign policy actor. In spite of a number of structural changes in the Lisbon Treaty (2007), such as the increased formal powers of the High Representative and the creation of a new institution (the European External Action Service), foreign and security policy is still in the hands of the member states.

In order to look forward, the European Commission conducted a study on the EU's global role with the illustrative title "A Global Actor in Search for a Strategy." The 2014 study concludes:

> It is imperative that the Union develops a clear strategic narrative for the future, if it still wants to play a major role in global affairs.... On the one hand, it needs to rest on objectives that reflect the Union's interests, values and goals in a coherent manner. On the other hand, it needs to base itself on comprehensive analysis of the evolving global order. (European Commission, 2014:7)

In June 2016, the EU approved a new global strategy called "Shared Vision, Common Action: A Stronger Europe." Compared to 2003 the situation has dramatically changed. The EU is no longer a model for the world, its very existence being increasingly questioned. The strategy itself was published a few days after the British voted to leave the EU. The contents of A Stronger Europe imply both continuity and change.

The EU will remain a global actor and a global security provider. The strategy nurtures a strong ambition of strategic autonomy. As before, it underlines the importance of an international system based on rules and multilateralism. The security threats have not changed but the focus is new. While in 2003, at the time of the Iraq War, the most prominent threat was the proliferation of weapons of mass destruction, the main threat in 2016 is terrorism (European Union, 2016:4).

In sum, the core principles of EU foreign policy during the Iran negotiations were effective multilateralism, support for international institutions, and the legitimacy of international treaties and agreements. During this process, the EU built the contours of its future role as a global actor in non-proliferation.

The EU as a Non-Proliferation Actor

The EU's response to the Iraq War went beyond the EU Security Strategy. The EU also approved its WMD strategy, which defined non-proliferation as one of the greatest global threats to European security:

> Meeting this challenge must be the central element in the EU's external action. The EU must act with resolve, using all instruments and policies at its disposal. Our objective is to prevent, deter, halt and where possible, eliminate proliferation programs of concern worldwide. (Council of the European Union, 2008)

Mainstreaming all EU policies—trade, development policies, humanitarian aid, research programs, environmental policies as well as foreign diplomacy—to meet the challenge of non-proliferation was—and is—a gigantic task. The strategy advocated adherence to effective export control mechanisms and the strengthening of the Nuclear Suppliers Group (NSG)[2] as well as the universal implementation of the Additional Protocol of the International Atomic Energy Agency's (IAEA) Safeguards Agreement. A related task was to secure all nuclear and nuclear-related materials. (Council of the European Union, 2003a)

The most challenging goal of the WMD strategy is related to a stable international and regional environment:

> The best solution to the problem of proliferation of WMD is that countries should no longer feel they need them. If possible, political solutions should be found to problems, which lead them to seek WMD. The more secure countries feel, the more likely they are to abandon programmes: disarmament measures can lead to a virtuous circle just as weapons programmes can lead to an arms race. (Council of the European Union, 2003a:7)

In matters of non-proliferation, the EU is often seen as an incoherent and weak actor with limited capacity to change a country's behavior. The EU was silent when India and Pakistan detonated nuclear devices in 1998. The EU has required a "non-proliferation clause" to be included in trade agreements with other countries. In the trade agreement with India, India balked at the inclusion of the standard clause, and the EU promptly acquiesced (Kienzle, 2015). Nevertheless, the WMD strategy, evaluated after 10 years of implementation, is seen to have promoted a more coordinated EU policy of effective multilateralism and been an effective catalyst for more intense European collaboration in the field of non-proliferation (Anthony and Grip, 2013; Kienzle, 2013)

The EU and the Non-Proliferation of Nuclear Weapons: Strategies, Policies, Actions is the latest and the most comprehensive evaluation of the EU as a non-proliferation actor (Blavoukos, Bourantonis and Portela, 2015). The framework used includes three levels: output, outcome and impact with performance indicators on all levels (2015:227). The authors judge the EU to be faring well in output performance, measured by the articulation of the WMD strategy and related Joint Actions and Council Decisions. They also laud EU priorities and the objectives of multilateral assistance schemes as clear and assess positively the EU participation in two nuclear non-proliferation crises, Iran and North Korea.

In terms of outcome, the EU has built an impressive set of institutional and financial capabilities to implement its strategy. Inter-institutional rivalry has been tackled in the post-Lisbon era by the European External Action Service. The only black hole in this generally positive output performance is the supply of international leadership. The EU is *another* actor, not the *dominant* actor.

In terms of impact, causal relations are difficult to assess in a complex system. Still, the authors conclude that "The EU has not been particularly effective in driving forward any policy solutions on the NPT's crux negotiation issues but has nonetheless managed to construct a niche role as a wholehearted proponent of multilateralism, which constitutes a key component of the Strategy" (Blavoukos, Bourantonis and Portela, 2015:236).

The EU and the Nuclear Non-Proliferation Treaty (NPT)

The legal base for the Iran nuclear negotiations has been the NPT, a voluntary, multilateral treaty signed in 1968 and a response to the fear that nuclear weapons would spread. The treaty, which entered into force in March 1970, has today 191 state parties. The UN Security Council is the ultimate judge on compliance with the treaty's provisions. The International Atomic Energy Agency carries out the necessary inspections and monitors the fulfillment of the state parties' obligations. (*Treaty on the Non-Proliferation of Nuclear Weapons*, NPT, 1968; UNOD, 1968; IAEA, 1972)

The treaty consists of three pillars: nuclear disarmament, non-proliferation and peaceful uses of nuclear technology. At its heart is a "grand bargain": The nuclear weapon states (NWS) committed themselves to nuclear disarmament and the non-nuclear weapon states (NNWS) committed themselves not to acquire nuclear weapons. Access to peaceful nuclear technology was affirmed as an "inalienable right." The balance of this grand bargain is viewed differently by the two groups.

The NNWS see the three pillars as equal. They agreed to forfeit the pursuit of nuclear weapons in return for promises of nuclear disarmament and for guarantees of the right to peaceful uses of nuclear technologies. A group of states, the Non-Aligned Movement (NAM), even see nuclear disarmament as the ultimate goal of the NPT. The NWS believe that non-proliferation is the ultimate goal of the treaty. The two other pillars, in their view, are "no pillars at all" but rather subordinate clauses to the non-proliferation pillar (Miller, 2012).

There is consensus that reform is needed, but what reform? According to Miller (2012:2), there are two parallel agendas for reform. The first is the agenda of Washington and its allies, which seeks to constrain the NNWS by limiting enrichment and reprocessing rights, tightening export controls, imposing more rigorous inspections, making the Additional Protocol compulsory, and making withdrawal from the treaty, today a legal right, impossible. The second is the NAM agenda, which sees existing safeguards as satisfactory. These states do not accept limits to technology access and guard the right to leave the NPT. In their view, the obligation to disarm has to be taken seriously, such as by negotiating a convention to prohibit nuclear weapons.

The need for reform is documented in the treaty's review conferences, which take place every five years. These conferences have approved action plans and steps to be taken, though with little result. Dissatisfaction with the treaty is aired by not approving a final consensus document. Practically every other review conference has ended without a final document.

The EU's special status in relation to the NPT limits its influence both on the treaty and the needed reform. Firstly, only states are party to the NPT. Consequently, the member states take priority and present their own positions before the EU non-proliferation official is allowed to give an EU common position. Secondly, drafting a meaningful strategic common position is practically impossible due to diverging interests. Two member states, France and the UK, are NWS. Four other member states—Belgium, Netherlands, Italy and Germany—have US non-strategic nuclear weapons stationed on their soil as part of NATO`s deterrence policy. Furthermore, the most active states for the NPT alternative reform agenda—focusing on nuclear disarmament—are also EU member states, namely Austria and Ireland. In addition, the EU is not the only entity that coordinates the states parties' positions. A number of member states are involved in different groupings active at NPT conferences such as the New Agenda Coalition.

The EU's Bargaining Power?

In spite of these structural limitations, the EU has promoted NPT reform on two critical accounts: the universalization of the Additional Protocol and the prevention of withdrawal from the treaty. Both can be seen as efforts to promote a rule-based multilateral system, where the same rules apply to all.

Although over 100 countries have ratified the Additional Protocol, it remains far from universal. In 2003, all EU member states had the Additional Protocol in force. The EU promoted adherence to the protocol at the 2000 NPT Review Conference through working papers and statements calling on countries to accept universalization. At the 2010 Review Conference, Brazil and a number of other developing countries opposed the move. According to Dee (2015:8), the EU was preaching to the converted. For many of the NAM states, accepting the Additional Protocol as a universal verification standard was a step too far.

The second case is about universalization of the treaty. When in January 2003 the DPRK announced its withdrawal from the NPT, it was a blow to the

EU's pursuit of the universalization of multilateral treaties and regimes. At the 2005 Review Conference, the EU position specified "that the EU would draw attention to the potential implications to the international peace and security of withdrawal from the NPT urging the adoption of measures to discourage withdrawal from the treaty" (Council of the European Union, 2005).

The resulting EU working paper highlighted the legal requirements, implementation and effects of any future cases of withdrawal. The paper underlined that any case of withdrawal could "constitute a threat to international peace and security" (in Dee, 2015:10). The paper identified the need for urgent consultations to ensure that the withdrawing state was in compliance with its IAEA safeguard arrangements. Further, any notification of withdrawal should be immediately addressed by the UN Security Council.

The EU position failed to make an impact. Divisions within the EU itself, as well as among the wider NPT community, over several procedural and agenda issues, resulted in the collapse of negotiations and the 2005 conference ended without any outcome agreement at all. Dee concludes on the two cases in relation to the EU's WMD strategy:

> whilst the 2003 Strategy has enabled the EU to promote itself as a strong advocate of the multilateral process in dealing with the proliferation of WMD, this has not been translated into substantive goal attainment or influence upon the non-proliferation regime itself. The Additional Protocol remains a voluntary measure and the NPT has still failed to adequately address the dangerous precedent that the DPRK set in withdrawing from the Treaty in 2003. (Dee, 2015:13)

Dee explains the results by the fact that the NPT Grand Bargain is deeply entrenched in the minds of the NNWS—and particularly the NAM—and that the EU has had limited powers of persuasion in asking them to commit to more.

> This in turn raises important implications for the EU as a global nuclear non- proliferation actor, and its ability to fulfil its objectives of a stronger, more credible and effective multilateral nuclear non-proliferation regime. For one thing, the EU's negotiation position within the NPT is itself a reflection of the imbalance of the Grand Bargain, not an answer on how to resolve it. If the EU therefore intends to play on its unique make-up as a group of both NWS and NNWS as a comparative advantage, it must first achieve the required equity between the NPT's three pillars internally before it can represent the sort of "compromise position" needed to lead the way within the NPT as a whole. (Dee, 2015:14)

This is, in short, the EU's past position as a non-proliferation actor in relation to both its own WMD strategy and reform needs of the NPT. I will return to these questions in the final chapter given the lessons learnt in the Iran negotiations. The Iran case is a case where the EU was instrumental in changing a country's behavior, in creating the foundations of its own global role and in applying the concept of "effective multilateralism" in practice.

Notes

1 Author's interview with a former senior EEAS official, March 18, 2015 in London.
2 The Nuclear Suppliers Group (NSG), a group of countries exporting technology and specifying guidelines for nuclear exports and nuclear-related exports. For more information, see www.nuclearsuppliersgroup.org/en/.

References

Albright, M. (1993) *Statement of the honorable Madeleine K. Albright, US Permanent Representative to the United Nations*, in US Participation in United Nations Peacekeeping Activities, Hearings before the Subcomittee on International Security, International Organizations and Human Rights of the Committee on Foreign Affairs, House of Representatives, Washington, DC: US Government Printing Office. Available: https://archive.org/stream/usparticipationi1994unit/usparticipationi1994unit_djvu.txt [July 18, 2016]
Anthony, I. and Grip, L. (2013) *Strengthening the European Union's Future Approach to WMD Non-Proliferation*, SIPRI Policy Paper, No. 37, Stockholm: Stockholm International Peace Research Institute.
Biscop, S. (2004) The European Security Strategy: Implementing a distinctive Approach to Security, Security and Strategy Paper, No. 82, Brussels: Royal Defence College.
Biscop, S. (2005) Effective Multilateralism and Collective Security: Empowering the UN, IIEB Working Paper 16, Leuven: Institute for International and European Policy.
Bouchard, C. and Peterson, J. (2011) *Conceptualising Multilateralism: Can We All Just Get Along?*, Mercury E-paper No. 1, February. Available: http://mercury.uni-koeln.de/fileadmin/user_upload/E-paper_no1_r2010.pdf [July 17, 2016]
Blavoukos, S., Bourantonis, D. and Portela, C. (ed.) (2015) *The EU and the Non-Proliferation of Nuclear Weapons. Strategies, Policies, Actions*, New York: Palgrave Macmillan.
Bretherton, C. and Vogler, J. (1999) *The European Union as a Global Actor*, Routledge: Taylor and Francis.
Council of the European Union (2003a) *EU Strategy against Proliferation of Weapons of Mass Destruction*, (15708/03), 10 December.
Council of the European Union (2003b) *European Security Strategy: A Secure Europe in a Better World, 12 December*. Available: www.consilium.europa.eu/uedocs/cmsUpload/78367.pdf [July 17, 2016]

Council of the European Union (2005) Council Common Position 2005/329/PESC of 25 April 2005 relating to the 2005 Review Conference of the Parties to the Treaty on the Non-Proliferation of Nuclear Weapons. *Official Journal of the European Union*. (L 106/32). Available: http://eur-lex.europa.eu/legal-content/ EN/TXT/?uri=CELEX:32005E0329 [September 5, 2016]

Council of the European Union (2008) *The European Union Strategy against the Proliferation of Weapons of Mass Destruction: Effective Multilateralism, Prevention, and International Cooperation.* Available: www.consilium.europa. eu/uedocs/cmsUpload/EN%20prolif_int%202008.pdf [July 18, 2016]

Dee, M. (2015) "The EU's multilateralist combat against the proliferation of WMD in the NPT: mirroring the Grand Bargain," *European Security*, Vol. 24, No. 1, pp. 1–18.

European Commission (2014) *A Global Actor in Search of a Strategy: European Union Foreign Policy between Multilateralism and Bilateralism*, Brussels: Directorate General for Research and Innovation. Available: https://ec.europa. eu/research/social-sciences/pdf/policy_reviews/kina26572enc.pdf [July 18, 2016]

European Union (2016) *Shared Vision, Common Action: A Stronger Europe. A Global Strategy for the European Union's Foreign and Security Policy.* Available: https:// europa.eu/globalstrategy/en/global-strategy-foreign-and-security-policy-european-union [July 18, 2016]

International Atomic Energy Agency (IAEA) (1972) *Comprehensive Safeguards Agreement,*(INFCIRC/153).Available:www.iaea.org/sites/default/files/publications/ documents/infcircs/1972/infcirc153.pdf [July 18, 2016]

Kagan, R. (2003) *Of Paradise and Power. America and Europe in the New World Order*, New York: Vintage.

Kahler, M. (1992) "Multilateralism in small and large numbers," *International Organization*, Vol. 46, Issue 3, pp. 681–708.

Keohane, R.O. (1990) "Multilateralism: an agenda for research," *International Journal*, Vol. 45, No. 4, pp. 731–764.

Kienzle, B. (2008) *The EU and the International Regimes in the Field of Non-Proliferation of Weapons of Mass Destruction*, Conference Paper, CARNET Conference, Egmont Palace, Brussels, April 24–26.

Kienzle, B. (2013) "A European contribution to non-proliferation? The EU WMD Strategy at ten," *International Affairs*, Vol. 89, Issue 5, September 10, pp. 1143–1159.

Kienzle, B. (2015) Integrating without quite breaking the rules: the EU and India's acceptance within the non-proliferation regime. Non-proliferation Paper No. 43. SIPRI.

Koops, J. (2011) *The European Union an Integrative Power? Assessing the EU's "Effective Multilateralism" towards NATO and the United Nations*, Brussels: VUB Press.

Martin, L. (2003) "Interests, power, and multilateralism," *International Organization*, Vol. 46, No. 4 (Autumn 1992), pp. 765–792.

Miller, S. (2012) *Nuclear Collisions: Discord, Reform and the Nuclear Nonproliferation Regime*, Cambridge: American Academy of Arts and Sciences.

Morse, J. and Keohane, R. (2014) "Contested multilateralism," *The Review of International Organizations*, 9.4, pp. 385–412.

Ojanen, H. (2004) *Inter-Organisational Relations as a Factor Shaping the EU's External Identity*, FIIA Working Papers 49, Helsinki: The Finnish Institute of International Affairs.

Ross, D. (2008) *Statecraft: And How to Restore America's Standing in the World*. New York: Farrar, Straus and Giroux.

Ruggie, J. (ed.) (1993) *Multilateralism Matters: The Theory and Praxis of an Institutional Form*, New York: Columbia University Press.

Treaty of Lisbon Amending the Treaty on European Union and the Treaty Establishing the European Community, 13 December 2007 [Online]. 2007/C 306/01. Available: http://eur-lex.europa.eu/legal-content/EN/TXT/?uri=celex%3A12007L%2FTXT [July 18, 2016]

Treaty on the Non-Proliferation of Nuclear Weapons, NPT (1968) (INFCIRC/140). Available: www.un.org/en/conf/npt/2005/npttreaty.html [July 18, 2016]

United Nations Office for Disarmament (UNOD) (1968), *The Nuclear Non-Proliferation Treaty: The Status of the Treaty* [Online]. Available: http://disarmament.un.org/treaties/t/npt [July 18, 2016]

van Oudenaren, J. (2003) "What is 'multilateral'?," *The New Diplomacy Policy Review*, 116, December 2002.

2 The Four Steps of EU's Nuclear Dance with Iran

The Timeline

In his State of the Union Speech in January 2002, President George W. Bush named Iran, Iraq and North Korea as constituting an "Axis of Evil." Later the same year, in August, the political arm of the Iranian dissident group, Mojahedin-e-Khalq (MEK),[1] announced that Iran had been constructing covert nuclear facilities in Natanz, and was developing nuclear weapons. In February 2003, an IAEA visit to Iran confirmed the existence of the clandestine facilities. In March 2003, the Americans invaded Iraq.

This is the context in which the negotiations on the Iranian nuclear program were initiated. The process lasted for 12 years, until 2015, when the final deal was agreed upon. The negotiations were tough, and all but frozen at times. Without proof that nuclear material had been diverted to military uses, the negotiations focused on uranium enrichment to weapon-grade level. Throughout the negotiations, the Western negotiators demanded that Iran suspend its enrichment program, while Iran refused, maintaining that to do so fell within its "inalienable right," according to the language of the NPT.

Persuasive Engagement (2003–2005)

After the 2003 revelations from the Iranian dissidents, the IAEA visited Iran and, backed by the EU and the US, called for Iran to sign the Additional Protocol[2] and to provide a full report of its nuclear activities by October 2003. The US called on Iran to renounce enrichment entirely. The Americans wanted the nuclear issue transferred from the IAEA to the UN Security Council.

A military attack on Iran's nuclear installations was on the table. The EU was keen on reducing polarization between the more militaristic policies of the US and the trenchant belief of Iran to its "inalienable right" to enrich. Viewing itself as a necessary counterbalance to US militarism, the EU sought instead to promote joint security interests as a way to assert itself as a major player in foreign policy and to strengthen the France–Germany–UK triad, which had been weakened by differences over the 2003 Iraq war.

In May 2003, Iran, fearful of what was happening in its immediate neighborhood, sent a proposal to Washington to initiate broad negotiations: beyond noting a willingness to negotiate on the nuclear issue, Tehran also offered to accept the Saudi Plan for Israel and Palestine and to end support to Hezbollah and Hamas (Farmanfarmaian, 2011:12). Washington did not reply. The US assumed that, after a successful invasion and regime change in Iraq, the neighboring states would also, inevitably, collapse (Cirincione, 2003).

In June 2003, the EU General Affairs and External Relations Council expressed serious concerns about Iran's nuclear activities and called for Iran's full cooperation with the IAEA. The issue was now on the European agenda. There was a general fear that Iran would be the next WMD problem to be solved by US military force (Meier, 2013:3). The three European foreign ministers, Dominique de Villepin of France, Jack Straw of the UK, and Joschka Fischer of Germany, wrote a letter to Tehran offering technical cooperation if Iran halted enrichment and implemented the Additional Protocol.

The three ministers—later dubbed "the E3"—traveled to Tehran and met with Iran's chief nuclear negotiator Hassan Rouhani of the Supreme National Security Council in October 2003. He told the E3 that Iran was willing to consider implementing the Additional Protocol and working with the IAEA to resolve outstanding issues. In return, the E3 should accept Iran's right to peaceful nuclear technology.

The E3 offered cooperation on many levels, including renewed European commitment to a "comprehensive dialogue,"[3] which had been suspended due to the nuclear activities exposed in 2002. The EU-Iran Trade and Co-operation Agreement (TCA) and the Political Dialogue initiative launched in 2002 would be continued once the overall relations with Iran, including the nuclear file, had improved. The E3 demanded suspension of enrichment. The Iranians refused.

Mohamed ElBaradei, the Director General of the IAEA, solved the problem. He defined "suspension of enrichment" to mean that no gas was fed into the centrifuges (Mousavian, 2012:111–124). The Iranians agreed to suspend enrichment under this limited definition. The IAEA Board of Governors, under Russian and Chinese pressure, labeled Iran's suspension as voluntary rather than binding. The agreement, which came to be known as the Tehran Agreement (October 2003), was acceptable to all parties, and was even palatable within the domestic politics of Iran.

The Americans objected to the letter sent by the three EU foreign ministers. The US disagreed with the EU's diplomatic efforts, believing that the European "unilateralism" would fail. The US policy was to isolate Iran, both politically and economically, and to report the Iranian nuclear dossier to the UN Security Council. The E3 had, if the Iranians agreed to the EU terms, promised to object to this. The US demanded the full suspension of enrichment as a precondition for any negotiations. The EU believed suspension would come as a result of—not as a basis for—negotiations.

Throughout 2004, the EU position became more ambivalent. The EU lacked a strategy that would reflect the attainable Iranian and EU objectives as well as a common framework for the negotiations that could be acceptable to all parties. Seen from the Iranian perspective, the question was about legal rights according to the NPT. Seen from the EU perspective, the problem was political, how to achieve an Iran without nuclear weapons. The Iranians came to the negotiating table with their national interests in mind, whereas the E3's driving motivation was to be the "good Samaritans" (Farmanfarmaian, 2011:17) for the international community.

The agreed definition of suspension—the halting of feeding gas into centrifuges—was not long-lived. According to a 2004 IAEA report, suspension extended to the assembly and testing of centrifuges as well as the domestic production of centrifuge components. A November 2004 Paris agreement between the E3 and Iran further clarified suspension to include even plutonium separation and related installations as well as all tests and production at any uranium conversion installation (IAEA, 2004).

With the new Paris Agreement, Iran agreed to suspend enrichment while negotiations continued. The E3 acknowledged Iran's right to peaceful nuclear program and promised to oppose the referral of Iran to the Security Council. There were proposals to cooperate in fighting terrorism as well as in integration of Iran to the global economy. Much to the surprise of the Iranian negotiating team, the Supreme Leader did not accept the Paris agreement as it would not allow even 20 centrifuges, the minimum required for a laboratory-scale enrichment program. In the end, the Supreme Leader agreed to continue suspension for three to four months in order to allow time for a development of "objective guarantees" for the civilian use of nuclear technology, as agreed in the Paris Agreement. This was, according to Hassan Rouhani, the Iranian chief negotiator, the last chance for EU–Iran nuclear diplomacy (Mousavian, 2012:150).

To save the negotiations, the E3 and the Iranians established a high-level steering group and a number of working groups for cooperation on nuclear and non-nuclear projects and political and security issues. These groups started their work in December 2004. Iran presented in January 2005 four proposals for the needed "objective" guarantees, based on compromises worked out by European and Iranian engineers (Mousavian, 2012:151). Instead of a counterproposal, the E3 wrote a letter to EU High

Representative (HR) Javier Solana complaining that the negotiations were not advancing as expected. The disagreement was about the guarantees. The EU saw the complete suspension of enrichment to be an objective guarantee. The Iranians argued that the IAEA monitoring would provide the necessary assurances (Kerr, 2005).

The US had been critical of the negotiations and frustrated as the EU refused to refer the issue to the UN Security Council. In March 2005, the US policy seemed to shift: Secretary of State Condoleezza Rice announced incentives in support of the European efforts (Kerr, 2005). The US would drop its opposition to Iran's membership in the World Trade Organization and support the export of aircraft spare parts to Iran. In return, the E3 would support the immediate reporting of Iran to the Security Council if Iran violated any part of the Paris suspension agreement. Furthermore, the US would accept the construction of the Bushehr plant, which it had opposed (IISS, 2011:26).

Iran tabled a new proposal in late March 2005. Iran would restart production of low-enriched uranium and supply political guarantees for the limits of enrichment and, therefore, potential weaponization. Iran further offered to ratify the Additional Protocol, to allow continuous on-site inspections, as well as a political pledge not to build reprocessing facilities (IISS, 2011:26). In turn, the EU would supply nuclear power technology and know-how and provide sales of (unspecified) military equipment. The Iranians wanted to avoid the referral to the Security Council and came with a third proposal in April 2005 focusing on some of the same items as in March but also on short-term confidence building.

The E3–Iran steering committee met in London late April 2005. The E3 promised to consider the Iranian proposal but would not accept this as a basis for negotiations. The E3 was delaying negotiations in light of the impending Iranian presidential elections. The hope was that Akbar Hashemi Rafsanjani, the leading candidate, would support a compromise (IISS, 2011:26).

At the May 2005 NPT Review Conference in New York, the Foreign Minister of Iran announced that Iran would resume enrichment activities. The EU warned that even a partial break would end negotiations and result in referral to the Security Council. At a final meeting in Geneva at the end of May, the Iranians proposed a compromise based on an earlier Russian proposal: enrichment would take place in Russia, where the enriched uranium would be inserted into fuel rods for the Bushehr reactor. The E3 refused and the Iranians agreed to wait for a final EU proposal until after the presidential elections. In July, right before the EU would submit its final proposal, the Secretary of Iran's Supreme National Security Council sent a message to the E3 suggesting both initial limitations as well as full-scale negotiations to uranium enrichment in Natanz as well as export of converted uranium for enrichment in another country (ACA, 2014).

In the beginning of August, the E3 was expected to present the final proposal. The *Financial Times* noted that the Iran–E3 talks were near collapse. The EU would fail to propose allowing any enrichment by Iran which would, consequently, resume these activities. Referral to the Security Council seemed unavoidable. The *Financial Times* further commented that the punitive action was being led by John Bolton, the new US ambassador to the UN appointed by President Bush while the Senate was in recess in order to bypass his confirmation to the position (Bozorgmehr and Dinmore, 2005).

Coercive Containment (2006–2010)

The EU finally offered a counterproposal in August 2005, a turning point in the negotiations. It called for "a commitment by Iran not to pursue fuel cycle technologies" for at least ten years. It suggested a store of nuclear fuel in a third country and for Iran to return spent fuel to supplier countries. In return, the E3 would support Iran's civil nuclear program, and provide a secure framework for access to fuel, practical cooperation on gas and oil technology, early conclusion of the EU-Iran Trade Cooperation Agreement, and even a commitment to work with Iran on regional security arrangements.

The newly elected president, Mahmoud Ahmadinejad, rejected the proposal as a denial of Iran's right to enrichment, despite the possibility of reviewing the question after ten years. In September 2005, the IAEA Board of Governors found that Iran was in non-compliance with its safeguards agreement, based on documentation dated prior to 2003. Already in June, an IAEA statement to the Board had confirmed that the investigation was not close to completion, as there were a number of questions about Iran's cooperation with the A. Q. Khan proliferation network[4] (Sanger, 2004). Furthermore, Western intelligence agencies claimed to have computer documents showing potential involvement in weaponization (IISS, 2011:28). Still, due to Russian and Chinese opposition, the IAEA Board agreed in September to defer reporting to the Security Council, though the path to this referral was now clear.[5]

In January 2006, Iran removed the IAEA seals at Natanz and Isfahan and resumed research and development work on uranium enrichment. The January 12, 2006 European Council statement by the E3 and HR Solana called Iran's decision to restart enrichment a clear rejection of the process in which the E3 and Iran have been engaged for two years, and concluded that the negotiations had reached an impasse: "the time has now come for the Security Council to become involved to reinforce the authority of the IAEA

Resolutions" (Council of the European Union, 2006). Later in January 2006, the foreign ministers of the United States, United Kingdom, Russia, China, France, (the P5) and Germany agreed that Iran's noncompliance would be reported to the Security Council.

In March 2006, the Security Council expressed serious concerns over Iran's nuclear program and gave the country 30 days to comply with IAEA's report. In response, Iran escalated its enrichment activities and stopped the implementation of the Additional Protocol. President Ahmadinejad commented that he "did not give a damn on UN sanctions" (IISS, 2011:31). The Security Council members disagreed on how to react. The US, UK and France wanted immediate sanctions. Russia and China maintained this would only increase Iran's belligerence.

China, Russia and the United States joined the EU in a proposal to Iran in June 2006 ("June package") reflecting some of the earlier issues. The main point was to offer a suspension of the discussions in the Security Council if Iran suspended its enrichment-related and reprocessing activities. Tehran rejected the proposal due to the suspension of uranium enrichment but stated that the proposal contained useful foundations for cooperation (ACA, 2014). The proposal, based on the E3 offer from the year before, added to it an offer from the US to engage directly and to cooperate on the state-of-the-art nuclear technology. Enrichment would be suspended but only under negotiations and could be reviewed again after international confidence in Iran's program was regained. While this was a generous offer, Iran did not believe that the US would ever decide that confidence was restored.

In July, the UNSC approved resolution 1696 stating that suspension would be mandatory under the UN Charter's Chapter VII,[6] requiring Iran's full cooperation with the IAEA and threatening with economic sanctions. Iran had responded to the June package announcing that it was ready to suspend enrichment but not as a precondition to negotiations. Iran also demanded the termination of the Security Council discussions on the issue. A new deadline was set for Iran to suspend its nuclear activities, this time by October. Secretary of State Rice even indicated that a temporary suspension might be enough to allow negotiations (IISS, 2011:32). President Ahmadinejad announced on September 28 that Iran would not suspend enrichment for even one day (Mousavian, 2012)

The Security Council decision led to a new phase, where an agreement was no longer possible within the IAEA framework. In December 2006, the Security Council unanimously passed sanctions on Iran. Resolution 1737 banned technical and financial assistance to Iran's nuclear and missile activities and froze foreign-held assets of 12 individuals and entities involved in these operations. The resolution was, in effect, a technology ban, limiting also IAEA assistance to Iran. The resolution was based on a stronger E3 draft which had also included a travel ban as well as restrictions on the Bushehr plant. The core of the resolution was political. The E3 and the Americans agreed.

The Iran nuclear issue was now a matter for the Security Council. Resolutions were unanimously approved and to be applied universally. In March 2007, the UNSC approved resolution 1747, which doubled the Iranian entities subject to the asset freeze and banned Iranian arms exports. On arms exports to Iran, the resolution only asked states to exercise restraint and not to provide financing or concessionary loans. For the Americans the situation had obvious advantages due to their veto power. Ambassador John Bolton had achieved his objectives. The IAEA Board of Governors would not be able to interfere; the matter was out of IAEA inspectors' hands. The Security Council had the final word and was, "unlike the IAEA, authorized to compel a country to comply with its orders" (IISS, 2011:237).

In the wake of the UN resolutions, there were further contacts and proposals for negotiations but no agreements. Research cooperation, even pilot-scale enrichment, was discussed between Solana and the Iranian chief negotiator Larijani during the fall of 2006. There was no agreement. The Iranians insisted on research level enrichment, the Europeans required cessation. In 2007, there was an effort by the IAEA General Director ElBaradei to find a solution to the outstanding issues. A work plan was produced and a number of outstanding issues clarified. Certain sensitive issues remained, however, and the work plan was never completed.

Contrary to the IAEA reports at the time, which alleged the existence of a "possible military dimension" to the Iranian nuclear program, the US National Intelligence Estimate (NIE) of December 2007 concluded that Iran had, indeed, had a nuclear weapons program before 2003 but that this activity had not been resumed by mid-2007. The 2007 report judged that Iran wanted to keep its options open and wanted to develop a capability to build nuclear weapons (NIE, 2007).

The Dual Track (2010–2013)

The United States expanded its unilateral sanctions regime in parallel with the UN sanctions, pressuring the private sector against investing in Iran and to "keep Iran at arms length" (IISS, 2011:36). Already in 2006, two Iranian banks were barred from any cooperation with US financial institutions. In 2007, two large German banks voluntarily refrained from activities with Iran. Later in the same year, the US targeted the Revolutionary Guard (IRGC) in a move that was deemed "the broadest set of punitive measures imposed on Tehran since the 1979 take-over of the American embassy" and the first time the US punished another country's military (IISS, 2011:36).

In 2008, HR Solana presented one more proposal. In addition to the incentives of 2006, he proposed cooperation in fighting drug trafficking, integration of Iran in the international community, and the prohibition of the threat of use of force in international relations. This was a "freeze-for-freeze" (sanctions in exchange for enrichment), to be in place for six weeks before negotiations, and to be followed by full suspension of both sanctions and enrichment during negotiations (IISS, 2011:37). With positive signals from Tehran, the US sent Undersecretary of State William Burns to Geneva to carry out negotiations, which did not materialize (IISS, 2011:37).

In 2008, Barack Obama was elected president. In his election campaign, he had promised to negotiate with Iran directly and without preconditions. He approached the Supreme Leader with two letters, indicated that the US would join the P5+1 talks directly and employed a more conciliatory rhetoric on the issue. Furthermore, Obama was open to question the Bush administration's "zero enrichment policy." France maintained its position of zero enrichment and the British threatened the Iranians that, if did they not accept the international conditions, there would be a much tougher position on sanctions. As the Obama administration was opening the door to diplomacy and declining suspension as a precondition, the Europeans resorted to tougher sanctions and suspension as a precondition.

Obama's new policy on Iran was quickly tested when, in June 2009, Iran asked for IAEA assistance in providing new fuel for medical purposes of the Tehran Research Reactor. Specifically, they needed uranium enriched up to 20 percent. Iran viewed the West's response as a test of their promise to supply enriched uranium from a third country. In October 2009, a swap deal was agreed. Iran had 1,600 kg of low-enriched uranium. Of this, 1,200 kg would be sent to a third country, enriched there, and then sent back to Iran as fuel for the research reactor in a form that would be difficult to turn into weapon-grade material (Meier, 2013:89). Russia and France would also participate: Russia would enrich the uranium and France would produce the fuel rods for the reactor. Notably, this October 2009 negotiation marked the first time US Under Secretary of State William Burns and Iran's top negotiator, Saeed Jalili, met in direct bilateral discussions on the sidelines of the meeting.

France, Russia, the United States and the IAEA met with Iran in October 2009 to discuss the deal. France and Britain were critical. A one-time swap would not solve the problem. It would mean the West tacitly accepts Iran's enrichment capability, though not to military levels. Amendments would be needed to the Security Council resolutions to allow Iran to export the low-enriched uranium. Germany, on the other hand, saw this agreement as a way to finally break the deadlock. The United States, too, was eager to seal the deal. The E3 agreed.

Although President Ahmadinejad supported the deal, his opponents denounced it as a sellout of Iranian interests. Iran initially rejected the involvement of France, with which it had a problematic relationship after the Eurodif rejection.[7] There remained disagreements on the details, including whether the material be sent from Iran all at once (France's position) or in several installments (Iran's). In the end, the agreement dissolved, mostly due to domestic opposition in Iran.

The aftermath of the October 2009 agreement collapse took on newly challenging proportions. President Lula da Silva of Brazil and Prime Minister Recep Erdogan of Turkey met Ahmadinejad in May 2010 and signed a declaration in which Iran promised to send the 1,200 kg of uranium to Turkey, to be returned to Iran as fuel rods for the research reactor within one year. The Brazilians thought they were implementing US objectives. To Brazil's surprise, the State Department rejected the solution. The US had plans for additional sanctions in the Security Council and the Russian and the Chinese were about to agree. US Secretary of State Hillary Clinton explained there that the deal was "too little too late." According to her, the Iranians now had more than 1,600 kg low-enriched uranium so the 1200 kg was not enough. Iran began enriching fuel to the 20 percent level in February 2010, justifying it as fuel needs for medical applications. In June 2010, the Security Council adopted resolution 1929, against the votes by Brazil and Turkey, approving additional sanctions against Iran. The new sanctions included the prohibition of nuclear weapon–capable missile development and an embargo on the import of heavy weapon systems (UNSC 2010).

Resolution 1929 acknowledged the EU's diplomatic lead and encouraged the High Representative of the EU "to continue communication with Iran in support of political and diplomatic efforts to find a negotiated solution." France had by now become an advocate for Iran's isolation, although the Spanish Foreign Minister, speaking for the EU presidency, stated that the planned EU sanctions had the goal "to encourage Tehran regime to return to the negotiating table" (in Meier, 2013:15). In spite of the calls for diplomacy, the balance between diplomacy and sanctions tilted more and more toward sanctions.

President Obama's outreach was complicated by Ahmadinejad's surprise re-election in June 2009. The election process was widely suspected of fraud, and the president, consequently, considered illegitimate. People took to the streets in what is known as the Green Movement. The Supreme Leader certified the election results, reformist presidential candidates Mir-Hossein Moussavi and Mehdi Karroubi were imprisoned, and a wave of repression with arrests of human rights activists and reformists hardened the political climate in the country.

The release in November 2011 of the IAEA report on the possible military dimension also worsened the already bad relations with Iran.

In September 2009, the United States, at a G20 meeting, revealed the construction of a new enrichment facility at Fordow, near the holy city of Qom. Furthermore, there were allegations that Iran had been working with detonators for nuclear weapons, thus calling into question the 2007 National Intelligence Estimate that Iran had discontinued its weapons program in 2003 (IISS, 2011:40). The US and the EU used this report as an opportunity to call for new sanctions. French President Nicolas Sarkozy sent a letter to his British, German, American, Canadian and Japanese counterparts, as well as to the EU, proposing an import ban on Iranian oil. China and Russia argued against new sanctions.

Russian Foreign Minister Sergei Lavrov suggested in a speech in Washington on July 12, 2011 a "step by step" proposal, a first Russian proposal in the process. The proposal was not made public but included as confidence-building measures gradual limits to enrichment and the implementation of the Additional Protocol in parallel with gradual lifting of sanctions. The proposal has been discussed without any commitments on either side (ACA, 2014).

Both the US and the EU approved unilateral sanctions in addition to the Security Council sanctions. While Russia and China opposed sanctions on Iran's oil and gas sector, the EU decided in July 2010 to prohibit investment and technology transfer to Iran's oil and gas sector and to add sanctions on trade insurance, banking and transport (Council Decision of 26 July 2010). In 2012, the EU banned import of oil and gas from Iran and imposed limitations on financial transactions (Council Decision of 23 January 2012). Negotiations had come to a standstill, although the parties agreed to meet in late January 2012 in Turkey.

When the EU foreign and defense ministers met in December 2011, they concluded:

> given the seriousness of the situation, including the accelerations of the near 20% enrichment activities by Iran, in violation of six UN Security Council resolutions and eleven IAEA Board resolutions, and the installation of centrifuges at a previously undeclared and deeply buried site in Qom, as detailed in the IAEA report, the EU should extend the scope of its restrictive measures against Iran. (Council of the European Union, 2011)

The Political Will (2013–2015)

After a freeze in negotiations the partners met with Iran in Istanbul in April 2012, in May in Bagdad and in June in Moscow. Both the P5+1 and Iran presented at these meetings step-by-step processes to create momentum towards a long-term solution. Iran emphasized its commitments under the NPT and asked for recognition of its nuclear rights. Iran was willing to cooperate with the IAEA on the "possible military dimension" but required that the issue be removed from the Security Council and that sanctions be terminated. The P5+1 in turn required that enrichment to over 20% be suspended, and offered technological cooperation but no sanctions relief. Nevertheless, spare parts to Iran's commercial airlines could be provided as well as safety-related inspections and repair of the aircraft. After a break of nine months, negotiations took place in Alma-Ata in Kazakstan on April 5–6 with proposals on both sides.

The 2013 Iranian presidential elections changed the game. A pragmatist, moderate candidate Hassan Rouhani won the elections, which had focused mainly on the catastrophic state of the economy. Although the main criticism dealt with Ahmadinejad's economic mismanagement, the role of economic sanctions was also visible.

President Rouhani was well acquainted with the nuclear issue. He had been the chief negotiator in 2004–06, negotiating the voluntary suspension and implementation of the Additional Protocol with the E3. Javad Zarif, his new foreign minister, had been the ambassador of Iran to the UN when Iran was referred to the Security Council. Furthermore, Saeed Jalili, Ahmadinejad's chief nuclear negotiator and the counterpart to EU's foreign minister in the negotiations, lost the presidential elections. When President Obama, in the context of the UN General Assembly in September 2013, talked to President Rouhani over the phone, the scene was set for more constructive negotiations.

Before this, already in 2011 the Supreme Leader had approved bilateral Iran–US negotiations mediated by the Sultan of Oman, Qaboos bin Said al Said, upon the request of Obama. After an initial meeting in March 2013, there were up to ten meetings in Oman, a process that was accelerated by the election of president Rouhani (Rozen, 2015). There, it was agreed to strike first an interim deal, to be followed with a final one. Both Iran and the United States had their proposals ready in October 2013. It took until the end of November to get the P5+1 approval, again with France acting the hardliner, demanding changes with regard to the heavy water reactor in Arak.

The Joint Plan of Action (JPA), the interim deal, was approved on November 24, 2013. Under the plan, Iran agreed not to further its nuclear activities. The P5+1 and Iran agreed to a two-step process "to reach a mutually agreed long-term comprehensive solution that would ensure Iran's nuclear program will be exclusively peaceful." This final solution would include the comprehensive lifting of UN and multinational and national sanctions related to Iran's nuclear program and a reaffirmation from Iran that it would never seek or develop nuclear weapons.

Furthermore, the final agreement would confirm Iran's right to peaceful use of nuclear energy according to the NPT, but not explicitly include enrichment as part of that right.

The nuclear program was frozen. The JPA allowed Iran to use existing centrifuges to enrich uranium to 5 percent. Iran was not allowed to feed any gas to centrifuges that previously were not enriching uranium. The construction of the Arak heavy water plant would be halted, and testing and production of reactor fuel were prohibited. Additional information had to be provided to the IAEA, together with access to facilities not normally covered by the existing safeguards agreement. Video records were to be transmitted from enrichment facilities on a daily basis.

In exchange, the JPA provided for "limited, temporary, targeted, and reversible" relief on sanctions. This included the repatriation of $700 million per month from oil sales, plus an additional $65 million per month for tuition for Iranian students abroad. Oil exports were to remain at the December 2013 level, and sale of petrochemicals was allowed, as was trading in gold and other precious metals. Medicine had been exempt from sanctions but as banks feared punitive measures by the United States, access to foreign medicine in Iran had been a problem. Now a special channel would be established for medical exports.

The first deadline for the next step was in July 2014, extended twice, with a final deadline in March 2015 for a framework deal and June 30 for the final deal. During the interim deal, the IAEA confirmed that Iran had generally fulfilled the conditions of the JPA.

The Framework Deal was concluded on April 2, 2015 and covered the key parameters for a final deal. In a fact sheet, the US specified its understanding of the JPA. Iran, in turn, produced its summary of the deal. The US specified that sanctions relief would take place in a phased manner "as Iran takes steps to adhere to the deal" (Samore, 2015:24). Iran's understanding was that sanctions would be removed the very first day of the implementation and "new cooperation in both nuclear and other sectors will start with the world the same day" (Samore, 2015:25). The US position stated that, if Iran failed to fulfill the conditions, sanctions would "snap back" into place. Iran underlined that the P5+1 is committed not to impose new nuclear related sanctions. A particularly sensitive issue was the possible military dimension and the inspection of military sites. As President Obama stated "if we see something suspicious, we will inspect it," while the Supreme Leader pointed out that foreigners are not allowed to cross the boundaries "to stop the country's defensive development under the pretext of supervision and inspection" (Samore, 2015:31).

The final deal, the Joint Comprehensive Plan of Action (JCPOA, 2015) was concluded not on June 30 but on July 14, 2015. It confirms the restrictions on Iran's enrichment program. The IAEA will monitor the stored centrifuges and related infrastructure for 15 years, and verify component inventory and facilities for 20 years. Even if the duration of many of these verification measures is limited, Iran's safeguards obligations are permanent. While these apply only to declared sites, a mechanism was to allow access also to non-declared sites "if the IAEA has concerns regarding undeclared nuclear materials or activities inconsistent with" the JCPOA (JCPOA, 2015:3). A Joint Commission will be established between the P5+1 and Iran to monitor the implementation of the deal. Potential nuclear-related exports will be subject to the Nuclear Suppliers Group's export guidelines and a special procurement channel will approve all transfers during 10 years. There is a special roadmap for clarification of outstanding issues, which will enable the IAEA to assess issues related to the possible military dimension.

On July 20, the Security Council adopted resolution 2231 endorsing the JCPOA. In September 2015, the US Senate Democrats succeeded in blocking a resolution disapproving the JCPOA. A few days later, the Iranian parliament approved the deal, and the Guardian Council confirmed that it was not in disagreement with Islam or the Constitution. Iran was now also ready for implementation. The IAEA issued its final report on the past and present issues (IAEA, 2015) on December 2, 2015 which the Board approved on December 15. The implementation of the deal was begun on January 16, 2016, the Implementation Day.

Notes

1 The People's Mujahedin of Iran (or Mojahedin-e-Khalq, known by the acronyms MEK, MKO or PMOI) was founded in 1965 and took part in the 1979 revolution that overthrew the regime of Shah Mohammad Reza Pahlavi, but was later suppressed by the Ayatollah Ruhollah Khomeini's revolutionary organizations. MEK launched a campaign against the new Islamic government, and fought with Iraqis in the protracted Iran-Iraq war (1980–1988), a fact that has caused Iranians to view MEK members as traitors. Both the EU and the US have listed the MEK as a terrorist organization. In 2001, the group denounced violence, and was removed from the lists of terrorist organizations, first by the European Council in 2009 and then by the US State Department in 2012.
2 Iran has been a signatory of the NPT since 1970. It ratified the Safeguards Agreement but has only signed, not ratified, the Additional Protocol.
3 The Iranian President Mohammed Khatami initiated a high-level dialogue with the EU in 1998 during a thaw of EU–Iran relations. The dialogue, which was discontinued due to the nuclear problem, was to cover issues ranging from nuclear arms proliferation and human rights to economic cooperation (O'Rourke, 1998).
4 Abdul Qadeer Khan is a Pakistani nuclear physicist and the founder of the nuclear enrichment program for Pakistan's nuclear bomb project. He had an active role in illicit proliferation of nuclear weapons technology.

5 By this time, although a Russian proposal to enrich fuel for Iran on Russian soil still lingered, confidence in such a solution was clearly waning by the September 2005 IAEA meeting. For more information, see IISS (2011:29).
6 The resolution to refer Iran to the Security Council was based on the UN Chapter VII, which meant that Iran was a threat to world peace. Russia and China had originally opposed a Chapter VII referral as they feared it could legitimize a military intervention. In the end they consented. The chapter states that the council shall determine the existence of any threat to peace, breach of the peace, or act of aggression and shall make recommendations, or decide what measures should be taken in accordance with articles 41 and 42, to maintain and restore international peace. (UN, 1945)
7 Eurodif was founded in 1973 as a joint venture between five (at the time) participating partners: Belgium, France, Iran, Italy and Spain. The idea was to place an enrichment facility in one country (France) and deliver the products (enriched uranium) to the co-financing partners, which would buy all their enrichment services from Eurodif. In 1974 Iran invested 1 billion dollars in Eurodif and was entitled to buy 10 percent of the enriched uranium. In 1990 Iran demanded fuel for its research reactor. France refused to deliver the fuel even though Tehran still held an indirect share in Eurodif. Iran views this refusal as proof of the unreliability of outside nuclear supplies and uses the Eurodif episode to argue its case for achieving energy independence by supplying all of the elements of the nuclear fuel cycle itself. France claimed that the contracts were outdated (Meier, 2006)

References

Arms Control Association (ACA) (2014) *History of Official Proposals on the Iranian Nuclear Issue*, Fact Sheets and Briefs, January 21 [Online]. Available: www.armscontrol.org/factsheets/Iran_Nuclear_Proposals [September 3, 2016]
Bozorgmehr, N. and Dinmore, G. (2005) "Iran-EU3 nuclear talks near collapse," *Financial Times*, August 5. Available: www.ft.com/intl/cms/s/0/9c20d694-054c-11da-97da-00000e2511c8.html?ft_site=falcon&desktop=true#axzz44OtIpCtZ [July 19, 2016]
Cirincione, J, (2003) *Origins of Regime Change in Iraq*, Proliferation Analysis, March 19, Washington: Carnegie Endowment for International Peace [Online]. Available: http://carnegieendowment.org/2003/03/19/origins-of-regime-change-in-iraq/ [July 19, 2016]
Council Decision of 26 July 2010 concerning restrictive measures against Iran and repealing Common Position 2007/140/CFSP, 2010 O.J. 195/39. Available: http://eur-lex.europa.eu/LexUriServ/LexUriServ.do?uri=OJ:L:2010:195:0039:0073:EN:PDF [September 3, 2016]
Council Decision 2012/35/CFSP of 23 January 2012 amending Decision 2010/413/CFSP concerning restrictive measures against Iran, 2012 O.J. L 19/22. Available: http://eur-lex.europa.eu/LexUriServ/LexUriServ.do?uri=OJ:L:2012:019:0022:0030:EN:PDF [September 3, 2016]
Council of the European Union (2006) *Statement by Germany, United Kingdom, France and EU High Representative on Iranian nuclear issue*, January 12.

Council of the European Union (2011) *Press Release*, 3130th Council meeting, Foreign Affairs, 17720/11, November 30 and December 1. Available: www .consilium.europa.eu/uedocs/cms_data/docs/pressdata/EN/foraff/126518.pdf [July 19, 2016]

Farmanfarmaian, R. (2011) *Iran and the EU: Re-assessing the European Role*, Centre for the International Relations of the Middle East and North Africa. University of Cambridge. Available: www.roxanefarmanfarmaian.com/wp-content/ uploads/2012/09/books-Iran-and-the-EU-revise1-April-2011.pdf [July 19, 2016]

International Atomic Energy Agency (IAEA) (2004) *Communication Dated 26 November 2004 Received from the Permanent Representatives of France, Germany, the Islamic Republic of Iran and the United Kingdom Concerning the Agreement Signed in Paris on 15 November 2004*, INFCIRC/637, 26 November. Available: www.iaea.org/sites/default/files/publications/documents/ infcircs/2004/infcirc637.pdf [July 19, 2016]

International Atomic Energy Agency (IAEA) (2015) *Final Assessment on Past and Present Outstanding Issues Regarding Iran's Nuclear Programme*, Board of Governors, GOV/2015/68, December 2. Available: www.iaea.org/sites/default/ files/gov-2015-68.pdf [July 20, 2016]

International Institute for Strategic Studies (IISS) (2011) *Iran's Nuclear, Chemical and Biological Capabilities: A Net Assessment*, Strategic Dossiers: Detailed Information on Key Strategic Issues.

Joint Comprehensive Plan of Action (JCPOA) (2015) Vienna, July 14. Available: http:// eeas.europa.eu/statements-eeas/docs/iran_agreement/iran_joint-comprehensive-plan-of-action_en.pdf [July 16, 2016]

Kerr, P. (2005) "U.S. offer fails to end EU-Iran impasse," *Arms Control Today*, April 1. Available: www.armscontrol.org/act/2005_04/Iran_EU [July 16, 2016]

Meier, O. (2006) "Iran and foreign enrichment: A troubled model," *Arms Control Today*, January 1. Available: www.armscontrol.org/act/2006_01-02/JANFEB-IranEnrich [September 3, 2016]

Meier, O. (2013) *European Efforts to Solve the Conflict over Iran's Nuclear Programme: How Has the European Union Performed?* EU Non-Proliferation Consortium: Non-Proliferation Papers, No. 27, February. Available: www .sipri.org/research/disarmament/eu-consortium/publications/nonproliferation-paper-27 [July 19, 2016]

Mousavian, S. H. (2012) *The Iranian Nuclear Crisis: A Memoir*, Washington: Carnegie Endowment for International Peace.

National Intelligence Estimate (NIE) (2007) *Iran: Nuclear Intentions and Capabilities*, Washington: National Intelligence Council. Available: www.dni .gov/files/documents/Newsroom/Reports%20and%20Pubs/20071203_ release.pdf [July 19,2016]

O'Rourke, B. (1998) *Iran: EU Set to Open High-Level Dialogue with Teheran*, Radio Free Europe [Online]. Available: www.rferl.org/content/article/1088860. html [July 19, 2016]

Rozen, L. (2015) "Inside the secret US-Iran diplomacy that sealed nuke deal," *AlMonitor*, 11 August. Available: www.al-monitor.com/pulse/originals/2015/08/ iran-us-nuclear-khamenei-salehi-jcpoa-diplomacy.html [July 19, 2016]

Samore, G. (ed.) (2015) *Decoding the Iran Nuclear Deal: Key Questions, Points of Divergence, Pros and Cons, Pending Legislation, and Essential Facts*, Cambridge, MA: Belfer Center for Science and International Affairs.

Sanger, D. (2004) "The Khan Network," Paper presented at the *Conference on South Asia and the Nuclear Future*, CISAC, Stanford University, June 4.

United Nations (UN) (1945) *Charter of the United Nations, Chapter VII: Action with Respect to Threats to the Peace, Breaches of the Peace, and Acts of Aggression*. Available: www.un.org/en/sections/un-charter/chapter-vii/ [September 3, 2016]

United Nations Security Council (UNSC) (2010) *Resolution 1929*, UN Doc S/RES/1929, 9 June. Available: www.un.org/en/ga/search/view_doc.asp?symbol=S/RES/1929%282010%29 [July 19, 2016]

3 Multilateral Negotiations, Bilateral Results

In 2005 the E3 negotiations failed to produce an agreement. This chapter looks at the reasons and explores the multilateral context that replaced the E3 and the EU's ability to reach effective results. While initial positions for the EU and the US were diametrically opposite, the policies converged when Iran was referred to the Security Council. Russia and China joined to form a coalition that survived until the final deal, in July 2015.

When Obama was elected president the policies of the US and the EU again diverged. Challenges were posed by Turkey and Brazil, who contested the multilateral approach of the P5+1. In the process the EU's role was transformed from autonomous negotiator to a practical facilitator as the final deal was arrived at in bilateral negotiations between the US and Iran. The chapter ends with conclusions on effective multilateralism, on EU foreign policy actorness and on whether it could have been otherwise.

Did the EU Fail in 2005?

In 2005, the E3[1] were at a crossroads on how to continue the negotiations. They could strike a deal with the Iranians if there was an agreement on objective guarantees for a peaceful program. The alternative was to succumb to American pressure and approve reporting Iran to the Security Council.

The Supreme Leader had initially rejected the Paris agreement, since the E3 would not even accept 20 centrifuges for pilot-scale research work. As the agreement later was accepted, the Iranians felt that Iran's right to nuclear technology, including enrichment, would be acknowledged. The Paris agreement was the first step. Furthermore, the Paris agreement reaffirmed the European commitment to prevent reporting Iran to the Security Council. For three months the EU–Iran working groups worked on compromises. On January 17, 2005, Iran proposed a package of 33 political and security cooperative actions including combating terrorism and a commitment not to produce nuclear weapons or other WMD.

Further Iranian proposals followed in March and April (Mousavian, 2012:151). Instead of responding to these the E3 wrote a letter in March to HR Javier Solana complaining that the negotiations were not going anywhere. The disagreement was about objective guarantees. The cessation of enrichment was the European interpretation of an "objective" guarantee. Iran saw the NPT, the Safeguards Agreement, the Additional Protocol—together with transparency and cooperation with the IAEA—as the only acceptable guarantee. Finally, in July 2005 Hassan Rouhani sent a letter to the European negotiators proposing that the problem be solved by the IAEA: "Allow the Agency to develop an optimized arrangement on numbers, maintaining mechanism and other specifics for an initial limited operation at Natanz, which would address our needs and allay [their] concerns" (in Entessar and Afrasiabi, 2015:22).

During the spring of 2005 the Americans were about to get involved, having from the start opposed the European's "insane" initiative. President Bush traveled to Europe in February 2005. In March, Secretary of State Condoleezza Rice informed the Europeans of US support of European efforts on Iran. She proposed additional incentives in the process, allegedly in order to put the blame for a coming failure on Iran:

> Washington recognized that a show of support for the E3 efforts would help ensure that a failure of the talks would be blamed on Tehran, rather than Washington. This would strengthen Washington's position to rally European support for sanctions if the issue was referred to the Security Council. (IISS, 2011:26)

John Bolton, then-Under Secretary of State for Arms Control and International Security, was already in June 2003 pursuing a policy of referring Iran to the Security Council. This, in turn, would enable imposing sanctions on Iran. The EU initiative had derailed this plan. Bolton was extremely critical of the E3 negotiations:

> Even if I agreed with seeking a deal with Iran, which I definitely did not, what was gained by pushing to engage now? Why not wait until Iran was referred to the Council, where we could put some pressure on them, rather than agreeing to talk beforehand? (Bolton, 2007:144)

The Americans went to great lengths in order to convince the Europeans that Iran was developing nuclear weapons. The "laptop" documents[2] had been shown to the Europeans and were given also to the IAEA. The political arm of the Mujahedin-e-Khalq (MEK), the Iranian opposition group, was extremely active in February-March, feeding information to the press that the Supreme Leader had allocated financing for three warheads and that Iran would have a bomb before the end of the 2005.[3] The Iranians in turn revealed plans to start the uranium conversion plant at Isfahan, a way of pressuring the Europeans to respond.

Faced with pressure from both the US and Iran, the Europeans played for time. According to a former senior EEAS official, the Europeans dragged their feet for too long: "The Europeans could go on forever. Enrichment was suspended. They were very comfortable. But the Iranians did not see it the same way."[4] Already during discussion of the Paris agreement in 2004, the Supreme Leader had suspected that the Europeans were playing for time. These fears were strengthened in the spring of 2005, and the Europeans were told that the Supreme Leader's patience had reached an end. If the nuclear working group could not show tangible progress, enrichment would restart soon (Mousavian, 2012:162).

Iran embarked on a diplomatic offensive. The Iranians met with President Jacques Chirac, who agreed to let the IAEA solve the problem of objective guarantees, although his advisors present opposed the idea (Nicoullaud, 2015–2016). Chancellor Gerhard Schroeder told the Iranian delegation that the issue had been discussed between the EU and the US and even if the Europeans accepted the proposal, the Americans would not. In April 2005 the French Ambassador to Tehran, Francois Nicoullaud, told Mousavian, the Iranian spokesperson, that "for the U.S., the enrichment in Iran is a red line which the EU cannot cross." The message was the same from political director John Sawers in the UK: Washington would never tolerate the operation of even one centrifuge in Iran (Mousavian, 2012:165, 173)

The E3 asked Iran, in a letter on May 2005, to continue suspension, and Rouhani agreed to two additional months. As the EU had not responded formally to the Iranians' spring proposals, it was agreed that the EU would present its final proposal in August 2005 after the presidential elections.

At home, the Iranians were under pressure. The Iranian public believed that Iran had accepted complete suspension without getting anything in return. In the presidential election campaign, the nuclear negotiations became an issue. Hardliners labeled President Khatami's team as traitors, spies, and tools for the West who sold out the country's rights and ambitions (Mousavian, 2012: 169). In June, Mahmoud Ahmadinejad was elected president. The E3 negotiators had chosen to wait until after the election as they expected Rafsanjani, a moderate candidate and former president known to support relations to the West, to win.

The Europeans came with the promised proposal on August 5, 2005 called "A Framework for a Long-Term Agreement" (ACA, 2014). The proposal included, among other demands, a ten-year suspension of all nuclear fuel-related activities. The Iranians rejected the proposal as inconsistent with the Paris agreement and as depriving them of their inalienable rights. The main criticism came from Larijani, the secretary of the Supreme National Security Council, appointed by Ahmadinejad the head nuclear negotiator. He rejected all calls to halt enrichment (Entessar and Afrasiabi, 2015:24). The Europeans called off the negotiations on August 31, 2005.

On January 10, 2006, the Iranians broke the IAEA seals at the Natanz enrichment facility. The Europeans concluded it was time to go to the Security Council and called for an emergency meeting of the IAEA Board of Governors. Chancellor Merkel, at the time visiting Washington, stated that "Iran had crossed a red line" (Bolton, 2007:322). The February meeting of the IAEA Board voted for a Security Council referral (24 in favor, 3 against, 5 abstaining).

The failure to reach agreement was caused by a number of factors. In the EU there was a divide, in 2005, between the diplomatic/administrative and the political level. The former saw US participation as unavoidable as the Iran nuclear issue was a "tete-a-tete" with the Americans. The expectation was that without the Americans on board there would be no deal. On the political level there seems to have been a will to conclude a deal. Two of the negotiating foreign ministers, the UK's Jack Straw and Germany's Joschka Fisher, have claimed that the US intervention prevented the Europeans from succeeding. Fisher is reported to have commented to Rouhani that the US prevented a compromise between the EU and Iran (Mousavian, 2012:165). On June 14, 2013 as Hassan Rouhani was elected president, the UK former Foreign Secretary Straw said:

> I'm absolutely convinced that we can do business with Dr Rouhani, because we did do business with Dr Rouhani, and had it not been for major problems within the US administration under President Bush, we could have actually settled the whole Iran nuclear dossier back in 2005, and we probably wouldn't have had President Ahmadinejad as a consequence of the failure as well. (in Morrison and Oborne, 2013)

Whether Ahmedinajad would have been elected or not is a question one cannot answer. Nevertheless, the nuclear issue became a factor in the elections, as the Iranian public believed that the suspension was for nothing. The following US assessment touches on the deeper reasons for the failure:

> On the one hand, the EU failure to resolve Iran's nuclear issue in 2003–2005 was mainly due to the lack of understanding of the role and importance of the nuclear program as a national and strategic program in Iran's domestic and international politics. While on the other hand,

the absence of a comprehensive strategy among the EU trio—Britain, Germany, and France—in dealing with Iran during the negotiations process also contributed decisively to the failure. As a result, not only did Iran lose trust in the EU's ability to facilitate genuine progress in the course of nuclear negotiations, but gradually and inevitably the EU was forced to leave its independent and mediatory role in Iran's nuclear dossier, take a tough line, and finally act in concert with U.S. policy. (Barzegar, 2010)

Years later, in December 2011, I met at lunch with Olli Heinonen, the former director of the IAEA safeguards department, and Ali Asgar Soltanieh, the Iranian ambassador to the IAEA. They were attending a meeting of the European Parliament's delegation for relations with Iran, which I chaired, to discuss the nuclear program. Our discussion went all the way back to 2005, the time after the Paris agreement. Both agreed that a compromise could have been achieved as a face-saving operation, if the EU had agreed to 20 centrifuges for research purposes. The final deal in July 2015 agreed to 5060.

The Multilateral Context: P5+1

The period where the E3 was the sole actor (2003–2005) ended quickly and ushered in the vision of the EU security strategy: effective multilateralism. Right before the Iran file was reported to the Security Council, the E3 were joined not only by the US, but also by Russia and China. They met for the first time in January 2006 at an emergency meeting in London.

In July 2006 the French Permanent Representative to the UN sent a letter to the President of the Security Council transmitting a statement on behalf of the Ministers of Foreign Affairs of China, France, Germany, the Russian Federation, the United Kingdom, the United States and the High Representative of the European Union. In the statement, dated July 12, the group noted that it had agreed, in June, on far-reaching proposals as the basis for negotiations with Iran, but the Iranians had given no indication that they would engage seriously:

> We have agreed to seek a Security Council resolution that would make the IAEA-required suspension mandatory. Should the Islamic Republic refuse to comply, we will work for the adoption of measures, under Chapter VII, article 41, of the Charter of the United Nations. (UNSC, 2006a)

Already on March 29, 2006, the Security Council, in a presidential state-ment, had underlined the importance of Iran re-establishing full, sustained suspension of enrichment as required by the IAEA Board of Governors. The statement also called for a diplomatic, negotiated solution that would guarantee that Iran's nuclear program was exclusively peaceful. The July referral created a group that was to negotiate with Iran for almost ten years. Surely, the group consisting of China, Russia, the US, the UK, France and Germany was a multilateral arrangement, similar, but not identical to, the Security Council's permanent members. Germany's presence indicated it was not institutional, but rather "ad hoc" multilateralism, a "coalition of the willing," where the E3 joined with the three superpowers.

HR Javier Solana remained in charge leading the talks, which seemed convenient for everybody involved:

> The Americans would feel comfortable, since this would spare them the need for being exposed directly—we were under the Bush administration; the Russians and the Chinese would feel more comfortable with an EU leadership than an American one; and the E3 could be sure that important elements needed in the package proposals to be offered to Iran could be delivered. (Giannella, 2012)

It was an arrangement with an ambiguous identity. Seen from the EU, the team's identity was E3+3, clustering the three EU states together and the three superpowers. In the final deal, the signature of E3/EU+3 underscores the role of the EU, not just the three European states. The rest of the world viewed it with a stronger Security Council identity—the P5+1—with Germany as the "plus one." The P5+1 formulation is here used due to its closer relation to institutional multilateralism, given the Security Council's final word in matters of proliferation and world peace. The P5 also represent the five nuclear weapon states of the NPT.

But why "ad hoc" multilateralism? Why include Germany? Germany was part of the E3 with an established role in the negotiations. According to a German ambassador, it was because Germany had the best relations with Iran and could talk to everyone.[5] Germany was an economically well-off country that potentially, if sanctions were later to be approved, would carry much of the economic burden. Germany remained in the group thanks to US support, and in spite of opposition from one of the European states.

While it was obviously functional to have all five of the Security Council's veto wielders in the talks, the group had no formal mandate. Since everybody, including the Iranians,[6] accepted this arrangement, it was not a problem. There was very little outside criticism and virtually no contestation of the group's legitimacy.

The lack of mandate was not a problem until the very end of the negotiations. In November 2014, Frederica Mogherini replaced Catherine Ashton as HR of European foreign policy. The European External Action Service, the EEAS, would have liked Ashton to stay on board as an advisor. In order to do so, the administration had to check the original mandate for the HR. A mandate was nowhere to be found.

Indeed, the Security Council never formalized a mandate for the P5+1. The first mention of the group appears in Security Council resolution 1696, sponsored by France, the UK and Germany, and passed on July 31, 2006, which states that the Council:

> *Endorses*, in this regard, the proposals of China, France, Germany, the Russian Federation, the United Kingdom and the United States, with the support of the European Union's High Representative, for a long-term comprehensive arrangement which would allow for the development of relations and cooperation with Iran based on mutual respect and the establishment of international confidence in the exclusively peaceful nature of Iran's nuclear programme. (UNSC, 2006b)

The second resolution on Iran (1737 passed on December 23, 2006) further welcomes the commitment by the P5+1: "welcoming the continued commitment of China, France, Germany, the Russian Federation, the United Kingdom and the United States, with the support of the European Union's High Representative to seek a negotiated solution" (UNSC, 2006c).

There are welcomes and endorsements but no formal mandate. In spite of this, the group remained active for ten years and maintained a multilateral arena for negotiations with Iran. The dynamics have been different at various times but the framework remained stable.

Coercive Multilateralism

Iran is reported to the Security Council on July 25, 2006. The first resolution, sponsored by France, Great Britain and Germany, was passed on July 30, 2006. The resolution (1696) calls upon Iran to take the steps essential to build confidence in the peaceful nature of its program, resolve the outstanding questions and demands, and suspend all enrichment-related and reprocessing activities, including research and development (to be verified by the IAEA). Iran had one month to comply with the requirements. In the case of non-compliance the Council would adopt measures under article 41 of Chapter VII of the UN Charter. This means that Iran would be defined as a threat to world peace. Article 41 allows for universally binding sanctions.

The Security Council approved in all six resolutions on Iran from 2006 through 2010, of which four implied sanctions on nuclear entities, sensitive technology transfers, arms trade and ballistic missile activities.

Iran objected to the resolutions and challenged their legitimacy by referring to Iran's right to a peaceful nuclear program. Furthermore, Iran challenged the legality of the Security Council's binding demands based on non-compliance with the safeguard rules. This was a responsibility of the IAEA and the inspectors, not the Security Council (Mousavian, 2012:225–228). The Council resolutions were passed in consensus, but not without some discord. While the Non-Aligned Group (NAM) had voted for the referral to the Security Council, they in their statements supported Iran's claims. On resolution 1747 in 2007, South Africa submitted amendments and stipulated "that any decision to lift the suspension would be based on the IAEA's technical judgement rather than the Security Council's political judgement" (Mousavian, 2012:273).

As for the P5+1, the policies of the US and the E3 had already converged during 2005. Also the newcomers, Russia and China, agreed to all the resolutions and the P5+1 were able to agree on common statements in the Council. The consensus was amazing. Consequently, it is necessary to look more closely at the positions of Russia and China.

Both Russia and China are convinced of the need to maintain a multipolar world order and are opposed to the hegemony of the US. Nevertheless, they did not object to reporting Iran to the Security Council. Both had an interest in an Iran without nuclear weapons. Aside from this, Russian interests have been geopolitical. The goal has not only been to counter the US influence in the Middle East. To be at the table with the other superpowers has been a confirmation of Russia's own superpower status. Russia was an extremely constructive partner during the whole process.

There were instances where the Western participants feared that other conflicts with Russia would tempt Russia to become a spoiler in the negotiations. The first case was the 2008 war in Georgia, the second the 2014 conflict with Ukraine. Yet despite the overall deterioration of Russia–West relations, fears of a Russian spoiler in Iran never came to fruition. This was the case even after Russia was sanctioned by the EU and the US after the crisis in Ukraine. A senior EEAS sanctions official commented that although he was in charge of the EU's Russian sanctions there was no problem in cooperating with Russia on Iran.[7]

The Chinese interest is mainly commercial, and China plays a key role in determining the success of any sanctions regime on Iran. China buys oil from Iran and has big infrastructure projects there. Scott Harold and Alireza Nader have summarized China's relationship with Iran as follows:

> Many countries are wary of Iran's nuclear activities and assertive foreign policies but at the same time attracted to its abundant energy resources and economic potential. Yet few have been as bold as China in

seizing these latter opportunities. As a result, China is in the paradoxical position of having more leverage than almost any other country vis-à-vis Iran, but also having the most to lose should more broadly punitive sanctions be imposed or war break out, a fact not lost on Chinese analysts and policymakers. (Harold and Nader, 2012:14)

On two issues Russia and China disagreed with their partners. The first controversy was about reporting Iran to the Security Council on the basis of UN Charter Chapter VII. Iran was defined as a threat to world peace and both underlined that this was not a mandate for military action. The second issue was the unilateral sanctions. Russia and China, although critical on sanctions in general, have respected the UN sanctions. They have been strongly opposed to unilateral sanctions and have not approved unilateral sanctions of their own. Both have maintained that the issue should be solved not by sanctions, but by negotiations.

In the Security Council during 2006–2008 there were a number of proposals, both from Iran and the P5+1 but no concrete results or even meaningful negotiations. The P5+1 maintained their demand on suspension both as a precondition and end result. Iran refused to suspend enrichment and increased the number of its centrifuges. There were proposals for multilateral action by Iran and Russia. Russia proposed first a joint venture with Iran in Russia and later moving enrichment to Russia. The proposals were discussed but there was no agreement.

Barack Obama's election as president in November 2008 was a game changer. Already during his election campaign Obama had declared that a nuclear-armed Iran would be intolerable. However, he had not made any commitments to the zero enrichment and preconditions policy of his predecessor. In 2008 there were, in Washington, several influential critics of the zero enrichment policy.[8] Thomas Pickering, former US undersecretary of state for political affairs, co-wrote an article proposing uranium enrichment on a multilateral basis on Iranian soil (Pickering, Luers and Walsh, 2009). In essence the zero enrichment policy had failed and the challenge was how to disregard it without emboldening the Iranians (Parsi, 2012:12).

The Swap: A Constructive Compromise?

New president Obama reached out to Iranians using the key concept of "mutual respect," which had also been at the core of the European early efforts. He spoke at Nowruz, the Iranian New Year in March 2009, and stretched his hand out to the Iranians. Obama's outreach got no response and was, surprisingly, not even welcomed by a united EU. Already in January 2009 the French had pressed, together with the UK, for new tough sanctions.

The French maintained that new sanctions would strengthen the hand of Obama in dealing with Iran. Other EU states disagreed and the EU decided to wait for Obama's first move (Parsi, 2012:13).

This came in June 2009 as Iran had asked the IAEA to find a supplier of fuel pads for the Tehran Research Reactor (TTR). The reactor needed fuel, enriched to 19.75 percent for medical purposes. The Obama administration, which had looked for ways to break the ice, saw the possibility for a win-win situation. Iran had 1200 kg low-enriched uranium (LEU). The US wanted to ship this out of Iran as a security measure. The Iranians wanted enrichment on Iranian soil. Producing the LEU in Iran, then, sending it to another country, preferably Russia, to be further enriched to the needed 19.75 percent and made into fuel pads for the TTR ("the fuel swap") could be a compromise.

This was the first new approach since Iran had been reported to the Security Council that seriously addressed the Iranian demand for uranium enrichment on Iranian soil and at the same time was a solution to the international fear of weaponization in Iran. It could, according to the Obama administration, be a confidence-building measure in order to start more serious discussions on the nuclear program. Negotiations were initiated under the chairmanship of the IAEA with participation of the US, Russia, France and Iran ("the Vienna Group"). The first meeting in Geneva was the first time the Americans and Iranians met face to face.

The potential deal carried risks for both sides. For the "West" this could endanger the desired endgame of zero enrichment as a deal could be seen as an acceptance of Iran's right to enrich. France and Israel were the hawks, while the White House also saw the risks in the case of no deal. Iran would increase its stockpile, which would reduce the chances for a diplomatic solution in the future. A US strategy was finalized after a meeting of the political directors of the P5+1 in September 2009. The Vienna Group met on October 1st in Geneva and a second time in Vienna. The proposal was that 1200 kg LEU would be shipped to Russia for further enrichment and sent to a third country (France) for fuel pads to be forwarded to the TTR in Iran. In principle the idea was acceptable to both parties. Nevertheless, in the end a deal was not agreed to.

The Iranians feared they would not get the fuel pads if the LEU was shipped first and the fuel pads were to be received only after a year. They proposed to get the fuel pads at the time of the shipment of the LEU or, alternatively, sending the LEU in several shipments with a share of fuel pads each time. The US, France and Russia would not accept any of these proposals. For the US the political value of the deal was to get the LEU out of Iran at once. The Iranians objected to French participation due to earlier problems with Eurodif. These conflicts were solved: Russia would have

France as a subcontractor, and the Iranians would ship the LEU out of Iran. But they still needed guarantees.

ElBaradei, the General Secretary of the IAEA, offered guarantees and an agreement seemed to be close. Both the Ahmadinejad administration and the Supreme Leader were in favor of the deal. The final failure is blamed on Iranian domestic politics. Ahmadinejad's opponents both among the conservatives and reformists argued against the deal. One of the arguments—that Iran was unjustifiably putting its fate in the hands of the West—was powerful and in the end the Supreme Leader withdrew his support (Parsi, 2012:147–148).

Obama's diplomatic initiative had failed and President Obama turned to the sanctions track. Moscow was frustrated that the Iranians did not trust them. In Europe, the states that supported further diplomatic efforts were disappointed. Further negotiations were deemed worthless as it would make the deal "even more attractive" to the Iranians. Some saw the result as a proof that the Iranians were after the bomb. The irony is that while the failure of the potential E3 deal in 2005 strengthened President Ahmadinejad's position, this failure weakened it. "No one wanted Ahmedinajad to get credit, particularly if this was a good deal for Iran" was a senior State Department official's comment (in Parsi, 2012:149).

Contested Multilateralism

The failure of the "fuel swap" was not the end of diplomacy, not even in this deal. Brazil and Turkey "stole" the negotiations and achieved an agreement called the Tehran Declaration. Turkey and Brazil did not intentionally challenge the legitimacy of the P5+1. They had both, individually, been asked to help and thought they were doing a service. Both had good relations with Iran and both feared war as a result of the diplomatic failure. Both saw that any deal that deprived Iran of enrichment was a non-starter. Brazil had given up its nuclear weapon program but its civilian nuclear program had met, in the 1970s, opposition in Washington, causing the country to opt for a secret civilian capability. "When Brazil looks at Iran, it doesn't only see Iran, it sees Brazil too" a high-ranking Brazilian officer is quoted as saying (in Parsi, 2012:176). For Turkey the prospect of a war in Iran was a threat as its planned economic growth at the time was based on stability in the region.

In 2010 Washington was working on new sanctions, both at the UN and unilaterally, as Brazil and Turkey were reviving diplomacy. While Obama was skeptical of further diplomatic efforts, the US strategy was to give a double-edged message: sanctions would help to achieve the fuel swap and keep the diplomatic option alive. The Brazilian president even received a letter from Obama supporting the "swap" as a confidence-building measure, an aspect of fundamental importance for the US (Parsi, 2012:187). The negotiations between Brazil, Turkey and Iran, in Tehran in mid- May 2010, were difficult. The core of the "swap" was that Iran would have to give up its right to enrich to 19.75 percent in exchange for the right to enrich at all. Iran agreed to place its LEU in escrow in Turkey, although the Iranians were skeptical whether Turkey and Brazil could secure the American acceptance of a deal. A parallel was referred to: they had once accepted that the Europeans could deliver the Americans without a result.

In the end Iran agreed to hand over its 1200 kg of LEU in one shipment and to receive the fuel pads within a year. The LEU would not go to Russia or France but would be under the IAEA seal in Turkey. If the West violated the deal, Iran could get its LEU back. The Tehran Declaration's first clause refers to the NPT confirming the "inalienable" right but also making explicit that this right also included enrichment (Joint Declaration by Iran, Turkey and Brazil, 2010). In a press conference the Turkish foreign minister called the deal a "historic turning point" and the presidents of Brazil and Iran declared that the world no longer needed to consider future sanctions on Iran. Both ElBaradei and Ban Ki-moon gave their blessings. In Iran the parliament gave its support and even critics of the government were in favor (Parsi, 2012:192).

The State Department was furious. The US had lost control over the negotiations:

> Indeed, Washington has interpreted the Tehran agreement as an act of defiance of its global authority, an argument which carries weight with other permanent members of the Security Council. Reluctant to see the initiative in important matters of international security slipping from its hands, the Obama administration has persuaded the permanent members of the Council to circulate a tough draft resolution demanding that Iran suspend uranium enrichment, and adding a long list of restrictions on Iranian military, commercial and financial activities. It remains to be seen whether this maneuver can succeed. (Seale, 2010)

The US did secure the approval of Russia and China of new sanctions—with major concessions to both—in the Security Council, just before the deal. Secretary of State Clinton stated at Brookings:

> They [Brazilians] have a theory of the case, they're not just acting out of impulse. We disagree with it. So we go at it. We say well, we don't agree with that, we think that the Iranians are using you. And that we think it's time to go to the Security Council, and that it is only after the Security Council acts that the Iranians will engage effectively on their nuclear program. (in Dreyfuss, 2010)

The other P5+1 partners also rejected the declaration in a common statement. The deal did not address the Security Council's demand on suspension (Westall, 2010). A minority in the EU, led by Sweden, favored the deal and resisted the pressure from the US (Parsi, 2012:197). The US bid for sanctions, resolution 1929, was agreed to in the Council against the votes of Turkey and Brazil.

The Bilateral Turn

In 2010 Catherine Ashton took the post of the High Representative for EU foreign and security policy. She had the ungrateful job of reviving the P5+1 negotiations after they had been frozen for most of the Security Council period. Meetings were held in Istanbul (April 2012), in Baghdad (May 2012), in Moscow (June 2012) and in Almaty (April 2013). Proposals (ACA, 2014) were presented, without any progress on the substance. The meetings were deemed successful if the date for the next meeting was agreed to.

During the final phase (2013–15), the multilateralism of the P5+1 turned bilateral. Both the US and Iran saw this as the only way forward. Only after the final deal was an astonishing fact revealed: according to a June 23, 2015 speech by the Supreme Leader, he authorized the bilateral negotiations as early as 2011:

> Through that intermediary [Sultan of Oman Qaboos], he [Obama] asked us to negotiate with them and to resolve the matter. I said to the honorable intermediary that we do not trust the Americans and their statements. He said, "Try it once more" and we said, "Very well. We will try it this time, too." This was how the negotiations with the Americans began. (Ayatollah Khamenei, 2015)

In 2011 President Obama found that his political space to reach out to Iran had become restricted. His outreach had been ignored, the swap deal was rejected and the administration was working with coercive measures much like his predecessor. Where was the difference?

The Sultan of Oman had offered mediation even before Obama's election. It was in 2011 that Obama first contacted him and asked for help. The Supreme Leader consented to the bilateral negotiations. The start was delayed due to divisions on the Iranian side and, later, due to Iranian parliamentary elections and US presidential elections. In March 2012, there was a preliminary meeting in Oman followed by a three-day meeting in March 2013. Here the then-Deputy Secretary of State William Burns conveyed the message that Obama would be willing to accept a limited domestic enrichment program if the deal was otherwise acceptable. The Iranian presidential elections had to pass before the final deal was conceived.

The EU's comprehensive, multilateral approach became challenged as the bilateral negotiations between the US and Iran gained momentum. The Americans and the Iranians would meet, negotiate and inform the others of the results. One of the former senior State Department officials commented:

> It is difficult to negotiate in a multilateral form. Seven entities is cumbersome as they all have to make a statement. Not only because of Jalili (the Iranian head negotiator 2007–2013), it is cumbersome even now when he is gone. The P5+1 has been an important surrogate for the international community, all five Security Council members, a kind of stand-in and more legitimate than the US alone. But it was very inefficient. The reason the JPOA (the interim Geneva agreement in November 2013) was achieved was because it was the US and Iran bilaterally. They produced 95% of the JPOA, gave it to Cathy (HR Cathy Ashton) who distributed it to the others. They were OK with it, only France was unhappy that they were not consulted. But without bilateral negotiations, no JPOA.[9]

France reacted crossly, criticizing the bilateral process and for having been left in the dark. Consequently, in 2014 the negotiations assumed a hybrid model. The core issues were dealt with in US-Iran bilateral meetings followed by bilateral consultations between the Iranians and each partner and finally together as the P5+1. While major issues were resolved between Iran and the US, other partners contributed with reactions and technical support. The bilateral turn is symbolized in the pictures taken after the Geneva agreement in 2013, which show Foreign Ministers Kerry and Zarif shaking hands. Only in some pictures is the handshake witnessed by a smiling Catherine Ashton in the background.

The negotiations came to a close when the final deal, the Joint Comprehensive Plan of Action (JCPOA, 2015), was agreed to on July 14, 2013. Iran's nuclear program would be restricted for 10–15 years in terms of the number of centrifuges, the level of enrichment, and access to research and development and combined with rigorous inspections. The P5+1 would continue to monitor the implementation with the EU as a coordinator. There is an innovation: the Joint Commission consisting of the P5+1 and Iran, which monitors not only implementation but also non-compliance. It has a mechanism for arbitration in case of disagreement and a channel for procurement of nuclear and dual-use technologies. Consequently, there will be a new institutional link between the IAEA and the Security Council.

From Negotiator to Facilitator

Initially, in 2003–2005, the negotiations were carried out by the E3 as an autonomous actor. The question is: why did Iran agree to negotiate with the E3 in 2003? In his book, Mousavian, the spokesperson for the Iranian team, discusses the alternatives from the Iranian point of view. In 2003, President Khatami, a reformist, wanted to negotiate with the Americans. The IAEA Director General Mohamed ElBaradei, after his visit to Iran in 2003, carried the message to Secretary of State Colin Powell that Iran was open to direct talks with the US. The proposal was rejected.

In 2004 the Iranians presented to the US the most comprehensive proposal ever. A memorandum, sent to the US through the Swiss ambassador to Tehran, Tim Guldimann, the official intermediary between the US and Iran, was intended to remove thirty years of hostilities and create a dialogue "in mutual respect." President Bush did not respond, and even reproached the Swiss ambassador of having deemed the proposal worthy of his attention (Shakir, 2007). Inside the Bush administration there were different views on how to react. Secretary of State Colin Powell and his deputy Richard Armitage were positive. Secretary of Defense Donald Rumsfeld and Vice President Dick Cheney denied an opportunity even for an internal debate by stating "we don't speak to evil" (in Parsi, 2012:4)[10] The US door was closed.

Iran's other option was the Eastern Bloc, consisting of Russia and China as well as states of the Non-Aligned Movement, the NAM. The Eastern Bloc was not considered to "have enough power to withstand the pressure from a cohesive alliance of the United States and the European Union" (Mousavian, 2012:87). Furthermore, Iran doubted the Bloc's ability to prevent the issue from being referred to the Security Council, a primary goal for the Iranians.

Between the non-existent possibility of negotiating with the United States and the perceived weakness of the Eastern Bloc, the European Union was Iran's best choice. The Iranians welcomed the E3 initiative and never questioned the Europeans as a negotiating partner during 2003–04. They hoped that if there was a deal, the Europeans could also deliver American support for this.

When the issue is referred to the Security Council, the EU's role changes from negotiator to coordinator. In the P5+1 the EU was the actor accepted by all as a coordinator with HR Javier Solana on the post in 2006–2009 and Catherine Aston in 2010–2014. A former American negotiator commented on the two roles:

> Solana was more of a facilitator, convening meetings. As a NATO Secretary he understood better that his job was to help out. It was a modest role. Ashton wanted to be the foreign minister of the EU and

play the role of a negotiator. This is seen in press statements: "this meeting was led by Ashton." The other member states portrayed this as a minor and less prominent role. But the countries stopped fighting about it. As the EU role became more prominent, Ashton did a good job. The US attitude was "who cares" and when the things picked up, the US had its bilaterals. It was OK. My sense is that in Washington there was a feeling that the only way the negotiations could succeed was if the US played a role.[11]

After the active Security Council period ended in 2010 both the US and EU had a dual-track policy, diplomacy combined with sanctions. Although the US took the active role in pressuring for sanctions, this is the only time when the people interviewed in the US see the EU as an actual partner: "we were partners, we needed the Europeans for the sanctions." For the Americans this is the clear focus of engagement with the Europeans. Those interviewed in the EU underlined that no one could have done this alone and—some added—without the Americans there would have never been a deal. Negotiations about the "fuel swap" took place first in the "Vienna Group," where France was active, after which Turkey and Brazil took over the negotiations. In both cases the action was outside the P5+1. In 2010–2013 the P5+1 was in a sleeping mode, although meetings did take place and proposals were discussed. The main action had moved to secret meetings in Oman.

In the final two years, 2013–15, the negotiations sharpened into a bilateral focus, and the EU role shrunk. The Sultan of Oman had overtaken the EU's role as a mediator. During this phase, the EU became a facilitator at best, as the substance was handled entirely by the Americans and Iranians. The EU's political director received instructions and took care of the practical arrangements. "But as things evolved, it did not matter," was an American comment.[12]

Conclusions

The P5+1 was an example of ad hoc multilateralism. It was not a formal institution, but rather a proxy of the Security Council's permanent members representing the five official nuclear powers established in the NPT. The presence of Germany was accepted. The group circumvented the veto problems of the Security Council, as consensus could be achieved through loyalty to the group before Security Council meetings. The group was amazingly stable from 2006–2015 and will have the responsibility of monitoring the implementation during the next 10–15 years.

Effective multilateralism is about results. In the Iran case, multilateralism was effective as a framework while results were achieved in bilateral negotiations between the US and Iran. The P5+1 created the conditions for the bilateral results. There is consensus that nobody could have done the deal alone: not the Americans, not the Europeans, nor the Russians and the Chinese. More importantly, there is consensus that the others could have not done it without the EU.

The support of the five Security Council members for the whole negotiation process and the fact that the P5+1 acted in concert lent credibility to the negotiations. There was no opportunity for the Iranians to introduce cracks into the consensus. This was particularly obvious when neither the Russians nor the Chinese vetoed the resolutions in the Security Council and when the US and the EU coordinated their unilateral sanctions.

The P5+1 was also an asset for Iran. Negotiating with the US alone would not have been possible without harsh criticism from the hardliners. The former negotiation leader of Iran, Sayeed Jalili, a hardliner, underlined this in the Iranian Parliament when discussing the JCPOA: "This point is noteworthy, that we never only negotiated with the Americans. We negotiated with the P5+1 because we do not believe America to be at the head of the world" (in Karami, 2015).

With hindsight the question is, could it have been otherwise?

The most far-reaching offer by Iran, at any time during the process, was in 2004. At this time, Iran's investments in nuclear technology were practically non-existent, centrifuges were few (none spinning), and research on enrichment was in a start-up phase. There was a reformist president, who had opened up a dialogue with the West and wanted to improve Iran's relations with the West. The Iranian proposal never received an answer, given the US policy of regime change.

Further, it could have been otherwise in 2005, if the E3 had accepted a small pilot-scale enrichment of 20 centrifuges rather than insisting that "uranium enrichment is the US red line that the EU cannot cross." Had the E3 presented a constructive compromise solution, the history of the Iran case would have been different. And what is more, the history of the autonomous foreign policy of the EU would have been another.

Finally, had the Obama or the Turkey–Brazil "swap" deal been accepted as a starting point for further negotiations a delicate balance between Iran's demands and those of the P5+1 might have been established. As a confidence-building measure this could have paved the way for further negotiations. Instead, the sanctions regime was expanded. As a consequence, there was in reality a freeze of negotiations for almost three years.

Notes

1 The initiative to talk to Iran is taken by the three member states, the E3. While the European Council discusses Iran at its meetings in 2003–2004 the formal role of the EU as representing the Union as a whole emerges in November 2004 when HR Javier Solana pushes his way to the negotiations (Meier, 2013).
2 A laptop was received by US intelligence with information on Iran's nuclear program. The origins of these documents has not been revealed. See Chapter 4 for details.
3 Associated Press, February 2, 2005 and Reuters, March 31, 2005. These allegations, while not verified, reflect the general atmosphere around the Iranian nuclear program.
4 Author's interview with a former senior EEAS official, May 6, 2015, Brussels.
5 Author's interview with a German ambassador, September 28, 2015, Brussels.
6 There was an effort by Iran after August 2005 to widen the group of negotiators to the East (India, Pakistan) to reduce the role of the European countries. Eventually the talks with the Europeans resumed and were taken over by the P5+1.
7 Author's interview with a senior EEAS sanctions official, December 8, 2015 in London.
8 In September 2008 five former secretaries of state (Madeleine Albrigtht, Colin Powell, Warren Christopher, Henry A. Kissinger and Jamer A. Baker III) called on the US to talk to Iran (Schweid, 2008).
9 Author's interview with a former senior State Department official, February 9, 2015 in Washington.
10 There is still some controversy over this issue. Guildimann claimed that the document detailing the proposal had originated from the highest levels of the Iranian leadership and that they were willing to negotiate. The counterclaim is that Guildimann as a source was questionable and the content of the letter not in line with availabe US intelligence on Iranian intentions (in Shelala, Fite and Kasting, 2013:34).
11 Author's interview with a former senior State Department official, February 9, 2015 in Washington.
12 Ibid.

References

Arms Control Association (ACA) (2014), History of Official Proposals on the Iranian Nuclear Issue, Available: www.armscontrol.org/factsheets/Iran_Nuclear_Proposals [July 20, 2016]

Ayatollah Khamenei (2015) *Ayatollah Khamenei Official English Website*. Available: http://english.khamenei.ir/news/2088/Leader-s-speech-in-meeting-with-government-officials [July 20, 2016]

Barzegar, K. (2010) "The European Union and future nuclear talks," Belfer Center for Science and International Affairs, December 4. Available: http://belfercenter.ksg.harvard.edu/publication/20582/european_union_and_future_nuclear_talks.html [July 20, 2016]

Bolton, J. (2007) *Surrender an Is Not Option: Defending America at the United Nations and Abroad*. New York: Threshold Editions.

Dreyfuss, R. (2010) "United States slams Turkey, Brazil over Iran," *Washington Report on Middle East Affairs*, August 2010, pp. 28–31. Available: www.wrmea. org/2010-august/four-views-the-turkey-brazil-iran-agreement-thanks-but-no-thanks.html [July 20, 2016]

Entessar, N. and Afrasiabi, K. (2015) *Iran Nuclear Negotiations. Accord and Détente Since the Geneva Agreement of 2013*. Maryland: Rowman & Littlefield.

Giannella, A. (2012) *EU Non-Proliferation Policy and Implementation*. Presentation given to the EU Non-Proliferation and Disarmament Conference, Brussels, February. Available: www.iiss.org/en/events/eu-conference/sections/eu-conference-2012-7b70/third-plenary-session-e310/annalisa-giannella-f32b [January 7, 2017]

Harold, S. and Nader, A. (2012) *China and Iran: Economic, Political and Military Relations*, Occasional Paper, RAND Center for Middle East Public Policy, Santa Monica: RAND Corporation.

International Institute for Strategic Studies (IISS) (2011) *Iran's Nuclear, Chemical and Biological Capabilities: A Net Assessment*, Strategic Dossiers: Detailed Information on Key Strategic Issues.

Joint Comprehensive Plan of Action (JCPOA) (2015) Vienna, July 14. Available: http://eeas.europa.eu/statements-eeas/docs/iran_agreement/iran_joint-comprehensive-plan-of-action_en.pdf [July 20, 2016]

Joint Declaration by Iran, Turkey and Brazil on Nuclear Fuel (May 2010) Available: www.cfr.org/brazil/joint-declaration-iran-turkey-brazil-nuclear-fuel-may-2010/p22140 [July 20, 2016]

Karami, A. (2015) "Iran negotiators defend deal at committee hearing," *Al-Monitor*, 2 September. Available: www.al-monitor.com/pulse/originals/2015/09/iran-negotiator-testify-committee.html [July 20, 2016]

Meier, O. (2013) *European Efforts to Solve the Conflict over Iran's Nuclear Programme: How Has the European Union Performed?*, EU Non-Proliferation Consortium: Non-Proliferation Papers, No. 27, February. Available: www.sipri.org/research/disarmament/eu-consortium/publications/nonproliferation-paper-27 [July 20, 2016]

Morrison, D. and Oborne, P. (2013) "US scuppered deal with Iran in 2005, says then British Foreign Minister," *Open Democracy*, 23 September [Online]. Available: www.opendemocracy.net/david-morrison-peter-oborne/us-scuppered-deal-with-iran-in-2005-says-then-british-foreign-minister [July 20, 2016]

Mousavian, S. (2012) *The Iranian Nuclear Crisis: A Memoir*. Washington, DC: Carnegie Endowment for International Peace.

Nicoullaud, F. (2015–2016) "La France et la négociation avec l'Iran," *Confluences Méditerranée*, No. 96, Winter, pp. 47–60.

Parsi, T. (2012) *A Single Roll of the Dice: Obama's Diplomacy with Iran*. New Haven: Yale University Press.

Pickering, T., Luers, M. and Walsh, J. (2009) "How to Deal with Iran," *The New York Review of Books*, 12 February. Available: www.nybooks.com/articles/2009/02/12/how-to-deal-with-iran/ [July 20, 2016]

Schweid, B. (2008) "Five ex-secretaries of state urge talks with Iran," Associated Press, September 15.

Seale, P. (2010) "The consequences of Iran's nuclear deal," *Washington Report on Middle East Affairs*, August, pp. 28–31. Available: www.wrmea.org/2010-august/four-views-the-turkey-brazil-iran-agreement-thanks-but-no-thanks.html [July 20, 2016]

Shakir, F. (2007) "White House 'reprimanded Swiss ambassador' for delivering 2003 Iranian offer for negotiations," *Think Progress*, 26 February [Online]. Available: http://thinkprogress.org/politics/2007/02/26/10643/parsi-iran-offer/ [July 19, 2016]

Shelala, R., Fite, B. and Kasting, N. (2013) *U.S and Iranian Strategic Competition: The Impact of the EU, the EU3 and Non-EU European States*, April 4, Washington DC: Center for Strategic and International Studies.

United Nations Security Council (UNSC) (2006a) *Statement by the Foreign Minister of France, Philippe Douste-Blazy, on behalf of the Foreign Ministers of China, France, Germany, the Russian Federation, the United Kingdom, the United States and the High Representative of the European Union*, (S/2006/573), July 12.

United Nations Security Council (UNSC) (2006b) *Resolution 1696*, UN Doc S/RES/1696, July 31. Available: www.un.org/en/ga/search/view_doc.asp?symbol=S/RES/1696%282006%29 [July 19, 2016]

United Nations Security Council (UNSC) (2006c) *Resolution 1737*, UN Doc S/RES/1737, December 23. Available: www.un.org/en/ga/search/view_doc.asp?symbol=S/RES/1737%282006%29 [July 19, 2016]

Westall, S. (2010) "Text: Powers dismiss Iran fuel Offer before U.N. vote," *Reuters*, June 9. Available: www.reuters.com/article/2010/06/09/us-nuclear-iran-response-text-idUSTRE6582W120100609 [July 20, 2016]

4 The Fight for the Right to Enrich

Since Iran has not tested nuclear weapons and there is no proof that fissile material has been diverted to military uses, uranium enrichment has, in the case of Iran, become a proxy for nuclear weapon intentions. Negotiations focused on suspension of enrichment and whether there is a right, according to the NPT, to enrich. Nevertheless, enrichment as such is not proof of military intensions.

Therefore, the enrichment line of thought has been complemented by the issue of "possible military dimension" (PMD). Research and development not related to fissile material such as tests with detonations, weapon designs and fitting castings into warheads become the focus in order to prove military intentions. These tests are not carried out in nuclear laboratories, but in sensitive military facilities, normally outside the realm of IAEA inspections.

This chapter explores these two strands: Iran's enrichment program and the efforts to verify military intentions. The chapter concludes with what is known on the Iran nuclear program and asks the fundamental questions in terms of the EU vision of effective multilateralism: Do the same rules apply to all? Are international rules respected?

Is There a Right to Enrich?

Iran has, during the 12 years of negotiations, never wavered in its conviction that enrichment is a legal right according to the NPT. No carrots of nuclear cooperation or economic incentives have been able to tempt the government to permanent suspension. No sticks of oil or financial sanctions have been painful enough to lead Iran to abandon enrichment. The P5+1 have seen enrichment, even on a pilot scale, as proof of military intentions and made suspension of enrichment into Iran's legal obligation in Security Council resolutions.

At the center of this controversy is the interpretation of a key phrase in Article IV of the NPT: "Nothing in this Treaty shall be interpreted as affecting *the inalienable right* of all the Parties to the Treaty to develop, research, production and use of nuclear energy for peaceful purposes without discrimination and in conformity with Articles I and II of this Treaty" (Treaty on the Non-Proliferation of Nuclear Weapons (NPT), 1968).

The content of the "inalienable right" has been the core issue. Iran has claimed that the fuel cycle, including enrichment, is a right. The US position has been the opposite, no such right exists. The Europeans have been in the middle, as particularly the Germans historically have promoted enrichment as a right. The E3 requirement of "zero enrichment" was due to the understanding that this right has been forfeited by Iran's failure to report nuclear activities and facilities. Consequently, two questions are built in here: Is there a legal right to enrich? Under which conditions, if there is a right, is this right waived?

The "riddle" of the inalienable right (Zhang, 2006:654) dates back to the late 50s, when the Irish proposed that states not already producing nuclear weapons should refrain from it on a voluntary and temporary basis. All states had the sovereign right to produce nuclear weapons, a right states would give up in an effort to prevent the spread of nuclear weapons. In exchange, these states would be guaranteed the "inalienable" right to peaceful uses of nuclear technology.

In the 70s Bertrand Goldschmidt, a former chairman of the IAEA Board of Governors, summarized the right as "explosion was forbidden, everything else was allowed" and that "nothing in the NPT prohibited Party States from following the technical path of their choice" (in Zhang, 2006:651). Consequently, in the 80s the European view insisted that the "inalienable" right was not subject to any restrictions other than the explicit ban on nuclear explosions (Zhang, 2006:651).

In 2005, an International Expert Group reported to the IAEA Director General on Multilateral Approaches to the Nuclear Fuel Cycle. They concluded on Article IV and the right to enrich:

> The wording and negotiation history of this article emphasize the right of each party in good standing to choose its national fuel cycle on the basis of its sovereign consideration. This right is not independent of the faithful abiding by the undertakings under Article I and II. But if this condition is met, no legal barrier stands in the way of each state party to pursue all fuel cycle activities on a national basis. Waiving this right would thus change the "bargain" of the NPT. (IAEA, 2005:12)

US negotiators have univocally maintained that while there is a right to peaceful uses of nuclear technology there is no right of enrichment and other nuclear fuel cycle capabilities. Wendy Sherman, the main US negotiator on Iran, has stated in the Senate Foreign Relations Committee hearings:

> It has always been the U.S. position that Article IV of the Nuclear Non-Proliferation Treaty does not speak about the right of enrichment at all. (in Beeman, 2013)

Secretary of State John Kerry maintained throughout the final stages of the negotiations that the right to enrich does not exist. Consequently, the final text excludes such a mention (JCPOA, 2015:3). Instead, the deal talks about the right to peaceful use of nuclear technology. Nevertheless, as the deal allows limited enrichment on Iranian soil, there is an implicit acknowledgement that the NPT does not prohibit enrichment or the acquisition of enrichment technologies. The Iranians interpret the deal as validation of their view that enrichment is a right.[1]

When Does the Right Become Alienable?

The "inalienable" right according to NPT Article IV is conditional to Article I (the transfer of nuclear weapons to other countries) and Article II (the manufacture of nuclear weapons). Article I was initially about nuclear sharing in alliances, particularly in relation to NATO and Germany, and has not been quoted in the Iran context. The manufacture of nuclear weapons, Article II, has been controversial in relation to Iran.

In, 1968 as the US Senate Foreign Relations Committee debated the meaning of Article II, Director Willian Foster (1968) stated:

> Neither uranium enrichment nor the stockpiling of fissionable material in connection with a peaceful program would violate Article II so long as these activities were safeguarded under Article III. Also clearly permitted would be the development, under safeguards, of plutonium fueled power reactors, including research on the properties of metallic plutonium, nor would Article II interfere with the development or use of fast breeder reactors under safeguards.

Nevertheless, the intentions were the final judge: "Facts indicating that the purpose of a particular activity was the acquisition of a nuclear explosive device would tend to show non-compliance." Two examples were given: "the construction of an experimental or prototype nuclear explosive device" and "the production of components which could only have relevance to such a device." The conclusion of the hearing was that it was impossible "to formulate a comprehensive definition or interpretation."

Later US efforts to define what is meant by "in conformity with Articles I and II" have broadened the definition of manufacture. Leonard S. Spector has argued that the NPT "commitment not to 'manufacture' nuclear weapons incorporates a prohibition of all related development, component fabrication and testing" (Spector, 1995). A State Department report from 2005 goes even further:

> The 2005 report states that assessments regarding Article II compliance "must look at the totality of the facts, including judgments as to a state-party's "purpose" in undertaking the nuclear activities in question". (Kerr, 2016:49-50)

The 2005 report concludes on Iran:

> The breadth of Iran's nuclear development efforts, the secrecy and deceptions with which they have been conducted for nearly 20 years, its redundant and surreptitious procurement channels, Iran's persistent failure to comply with its obligations to report to the IAEA and to apply safeguards to such activities, and the lack of a reasonable economic justification for this program leads us to conclude that Iran is pursuing an effort to manufacture nuclear weapons, and has sought and received assistance in this effort in violation of article II of the NPT. (Department of State, 2005)

Today there is no clear conclusion on Article II. Scholars and law experts have debated whether Article II implies a narrow or a broader definition of manufacture (Jonas, 2014). The conclusions lean towards a narrow definition. According to this, Iran has not been in breach of Article II (Joyner, 2011). Nor has the Security Council ever declared such a breach. Iran has been reported to the Security Council for its violations of the IAEA safeguards agreement, that is, Article III. This Article requires that non-nuclear weapon state parties to the NPT accept safeguards in order to "prevent the diversion of nuclear energy from peaceful uses to nuclear weapons" and that all sources of nuclear material have to be under control anywhere in the state. Further Article III implementation has to comply with Article IV and not hamper economic and technical development.

The "inalienable right" is not conditional to Article III but there is a clear link. In order to benefit from this right you have to be in "good standing," and nuclear activities and facilities have to be safeguarded. Nevertheless, there is ambiguity. Is it enough that they are safeguarded? Are there reporting failures which forfeit the right to enrich? Do all the outstanding issues have to be clarified?

In summary, the right to enrich is sovereign right, not given but confirmed by article IV. When a state (with the exception of the P5) ratifies the NPT this right becomes limited by what is seen as "manufacture", the rest is free. Facilities and activities have to be under safeguards. Reporting failures are judged by the the IAEA and ultimately by the UNSC.

Enrichment and Its Suspension

As a military power, we know that enrichment is the first step toward a weapon. The militarization side is easier to hide, so the enrichment is really the critical step.

The above is a comment by the Ambassador Araud, a French veteran of the Iran nuclear file, in a recent interview with the Arms Control Association (in Davenport and Philipp, 2016).

The most persistent requirement in the Iran negotiations has been the suspension of uranium enrichment. The Bush administration insisted on suspension as a precondition for negotiations. The E3 saw suspension of enrichment as the final "objective" guarantee. The Iranians accepted only temporary and voluntary suspension. Suspension of Iran's enrichment program became an obligation after the September 2003 Board of Governors resolution. This required that all enrichment activities be suspended immediately (IAEA, 2003a: 2). In the first Security Council resolution on Iran (1696) this suspension turned into a legally binding requirement for Iran, its "international obligation."

The first conflict in the negotiations was over how to define suspension. In October 2003, Mohammed ElBaradei, the IAEA Director General, arrived in Tehran. He called for the suspension of Iran's nuclear fuel cycle activities. Hassan Rouhani, the head of the National Security Council, was not willing to accept suspension. ElBaradei proposed a limited definition: if Iran avoided the introduction of uranium hexafluoride gas into centrifuges, this could be considered as suspension (ElBaradei, 2011).

At a later October meeting, when the E3 were in Tehran, suspension became a controversial issue. The E3 did not agree with ElBaradei's definition. The Iranians had been assured that this limited definition would be enough to satisfy the IAEA. Negotiations were about to break down. The E3 ministers were on the verge of cancelling the planned meeting with President Khatami and leaving for the airport. Phone calls were made to Khatami and to the Supreme Leader and the negotiations continued until Iran agreed to temporarily and voluntarily suspend enrichment (Mousavian, 2012:102).

In November 2003, after heavy pressure on ElBaradei from the US and the E3, the IAEA presented a non-paper (Mousavian, 2012:124), which introduced a much broader definition. While ElBaradei's definition was technical, the E3 opted for a more political definition. Enrichment suspension was no longer only a question of not feeding gas into centrifuges. Suspension included the production of centrifuge parts and their assembly and even the construction of related facilities. This was well beyond the terms set in the ElBaradei–Rouhani agreement, which shocked the Iranians.

In the early agreements with Iran, the E3 had accepted Iran's right to a peaceful nuclear program. When the E3 required enrichment suspension, it in turn proposed to guarantee the security of a fuel supply. Normally, enriched uranium is bought on the market under the rules of the Nuclear Suppliers Group (NSG). Iran has, since its revolution, been under technology denial, long before the exposure of the nuclear program in 2002 (see Chapter 5). It is not very likely that Iran would have been able to buy on the open market. Whether an EU guarantee would have made a difference was never tested.

An alternative solution would have been to move enrichment to another country. In the Iran case the obvious solution is Russia, given Russia–Iran cooperation on Bushehr. This was proposed and discussed seriously in 2005–2006. To be dependent on Russia was in the end not acceptable to Iran and Iran insisted on enrichment on Iranian soil. The "swap deal" of 2010 negotiated first by the Obama administration and later by Turkey/Brazil is illustrative of the Iranian position. It was an acceptable compromise. Enrichment to low levels would take place in Iran, and LEU would be transported to Russia and further enriched to 20 percent to provide fuel for the Tehran Research Reactor. Iran would enrich on its soil, but higher levels of enrichment would be carried out by Russia.

Multinational nuclear fuel banks have been proposed as a solution in order not to depend on one country and to avoid political conflicts that prevent access to fuel. This idea, which has been around since the late 40s, is one where the supply of fuel for peaceful uses is guaranteed under multilateral control or under the control of the IAEA.[2] The goal is to discourage countries like Iran from investing resources in enrichment of their own. As access to fuel from a multilateral bank would require the recipient country be in good standing, a country like Iran, under suspicions of military intentions, would not be eligible. Furthermore, according to a legal opinion from 2005, countries cannot be forced to buy from a bank (IAEA, 2005).

Verifying Military Intensions

The Swedish example (Acton, 2009) illustrates the problems of military intentions in a nuclear program. In 1958, Sweden developed a nuclear policy of "deciding not to decide." Swedish researchers conducted extensive nuclear research, while being formally forbidden to cross the line into research explicitly conducted to build a bomb. They produced knowledge relevant to the manufacture of nuclear weapons and prevented existing knowledge from being lost. Finally, in the 70s, Sweden decided to discontinue its nuclear program. The point is that there is no simple Yes or No answer to the question of a military intent on the research level. Many technologies have both civilian and military uses, nuclear technology being one example.

Furthermore, there are often competing interests within a state. In Sweden the ruling Social Democrats were generally opposed to nuclear weapons, while the Swedish military supported the idea and continued (with the government's permission) to carry out research. This is no doubt also the situation in Iran. The Supreme Leader, the government, the parliament, the Guardian Council, the Armed Forces and the Revolutionary Guards most likely have their own understanding of whether the country should acquire nuclear weapons. Acton's point is that the whole concept of a state having well-defined intentions is problematic.

Uranium enrichment, even on a large scale, is not proof of military intentions. A number of countries[3] enrich and are not suspected of harboring clandestine nuclear weapons programs. Military intentions must be confirmed by other means. Iran has not conducted any nuclear explosion tests and has not acquired any nuclear explosive devices. Nor had it made any decision to acquire such a device according to a US assessment (NIE 2007). The IAEA has not detected that nuclear material has been diverted to military uses.

Iran has not made a decision to weaponize, but international suspicions of military intentions have been strong. The indicators used have been high-explosive testing, nuclear warhead designs and casting experiments as well as the presence of and experiments with materials necessary in the process. Information on these indicators has to be sought out not in nuclear facilities, but in military laboratories, facilities and sites normally outside the reach of IAEA weapon inspectors. Judgments are often based on secret intelligence information, which makes a transparent analysis difficult, if not impossible.

The IAEA's authority to assess military intentions in relation to criteria other than the diversion of nuclear material to military uses is limited. The IAEA does not have the mandate or the technical expertise to judge whether casting experiments or explosion tests are proofs of military intentions. Accordingly, ElBaradei, in a report to the IAEA Board in 2006 stated that "absent some nexus to nuclear material the agency's legal authority to pursue the verification of possible nuclear weapons related activity is limited" (Kerr, 2016:4).

On the other hand, having access to the fuel cycle brings a state closer to the potential acquisition of nuclear weapons. In the early NPT negotiations this was called "nuclear pregnancy" (Rosecrance, 1968). "Breakout time" is the time it takes to give birth, from pregnancy to the actual production of a bomb. In the final phases of the Iran negotiations breakout time has been the critical criterion. Calculations were made, and the P5+1 countries disagreed, with France on the tough side. The JCPOA is based on a breakout time of one year for the ability to build a bomb, not including the ability to deliver a bomb.

The Possible Military Dimension: The Sources

After the press conference in 2002, which exposed Iran's clandestine nuclear facilities, the IAEA sent an inspection team to the Tehran Research Reactor, Natanz and other facilities. Iran provided information on its research activities with uranium conversion and laboratory and bench-scale experiments not previously provided to the IAEA. The report concludes that:

> Iran's nuclear program had consisted of the complete front end of the nuclear fuel cycle and that Iran had failed to report a large number of conversion, fabrication and irradiation activities, involving nuclear material, including the separation of small amount of plutonium. (IAEA, 2003b)

The 2011 IAEA report on Iran (IAEA, 2011) provides a complete list in an Annex on activities relevant to the development of an explosive nuclear device. Special attention is given to an explosive containment vessel for hydrodynamic experiments at the Parchin military site, identified by the IAEA only in 2011 but installed already in 2000.

The conclusion of the report was the same. All declared nuclear material is accounted for and the Agency did not detect any diversion of nuclear material; nonetheless, the Agency was not "in the position to conclude that there are not any undeclared nuclear materials or activities in Iran" (IAEA, 2011).

The US National Intelligence Estimates, or NIE, provides a view of the possible military dimension on another level. It assigns a confidence level to certain developments as a background for US policy planning. While the 2005 NIE assessed with high confidence that Iran was determined to develop nuclear weapons, the November 2007 NIE radically departed from this assessment. The key judgments were the following (NIE, 2007):

• Until the fall of 2003, Iranian military entities were working under government direction to develop nuclear weapons (high confidence).
• These activities were halted for several years (high confidence) and Tehran had not restarted these activities as of mid-2007 (moderate confidence).

- Tehran's decision to halt its nuclear weapons program suggests it is less determined to develop nuclear weapons than judged in 2005.
- Iran does not have currently a nuclear weapon (moderate to high confidence).

Iranian entities, the NIE stated, continue to develop a range of capabilities that could be applied in the production of a nuclear weapons, if a decision to do so was made. The NIE drew an important conclusion on how this decision would be made:

> Our assessment that Iran halted the program in 2003 primarily in response to international pressure indicates that Tehran's decisions are guided by a cost-benefit approach rather than a rush to a weapon irrespective of the political, economic and military costs. This, in turn, suggests that some combination of threats of intensified international scrutiny and pressures, along with opportunities for Iran to achieve its security, prestige, and goals for regional influence in other ways might—if perceived by Iran's leaders as credible—prompt Tehran to extend the current halt to its nuclear weapons program. It is difficult to specify what such a combination might be. (NIE, 2007)

Robert Gates, who was US Secretary of Defense at the time, states in his memoirs that he supported the publishing of the unclassified version of the key findings, even if they were contrary to the government's policy, as he expected it to be leaked anyway. He comments further:

> In my entire career in intelligence, I believe no single estimate ever did more harm to U.S. security interests and diplomatic efforts. (Gates, 2014:186)

According to him, most governments of the world wondered why the Bush administration would release an assessment that was totally at odds with the government's diplomatic efforts. His French counterpart saw this "like a hair in the soup" (Gates, 2014:186).

The report did not result in changes in US policy, but after the publication US officials consistently reiterated that Tehran had not yet decided to build a bomb (Kerr, 2016:58). Later National Intelligence reports confirmed the absence of hard evidence that Iran decided to build a nuclear bomb. In Senate testimony on January 31, 2012, the director of national intelligence James R. Clapper stated explicitly that "American officials believe that Iran is preserving its options for a nuclear weapon, but that is no evidence that it had made a decision on making a concerted effort to build a weapon" (Senate Select Committee on Intelligence Hearing, 2012).

The Laptop: The Secret Source

In 2004, right after the Paris agreement, a laptop found its way to the US government. It contained material on missile entry vehicles, high explosive testing of detonators, and a uranium conversion system. The stories of its origins vary. According to one story, the origin was an Iranian engineer recruited as a spy, and the documents came from a secret nuclear weapons program he had been working on. According to another story, the source was a German spy who stole it from somebody in a nuclear weapons project. A third story refers to a businessman building nuclear facilities and recruited by German intelligence (Porter, 2014:192). Officials interviewed "did not know the source or whether the individual was connected with the Iranian armed opposition group Muhajedin-e-Khalq (MEK)" (Dafna, 2004). A senior German political appointee and member of the German parliament Karsten Voigt warned at the time about the MEK as the origin of the documents. His statement was later verified by a source close to the German chancellor and foreign minister (Porter, 2014:194).

In the IAEA, the laptop documentation was treated with care:

> The investigation into Iran's past relies on a set of intelligence documents given to the IAEA that allege weapons experiments were conducted. Former IAEA directors including Sweden's Hans Blix and Egypt's Mohamed Elbaradei, as well as ex-agency inspectors, have been critical about the quality of the information. Iran says the documents are fake. (Tirone, 2014)

Tariq Rauf, the former Head of the Verification and Security Policy Coordination of the IAEA and Robert Kelley, a veteran of the Iraqi inspections of the US Department of Energy, both now at SIPRI, assess the "possible military dimension" in the following way:

> The IAEA's case on "possible military dimensions" (PMD) to Iran's nuclear programme is based primarily on intelligence information provided to the Agency by a handful of its Member States that cleverly distributed the information amongst themselves and drip fed it to the Agency over a period of time. The initial information on PMD was made available in electronic form around 2005—this was digital information purported to be from Iranian nuclear and defense establishments. No hard copies of the original documentation were ever provided to the Agency which made its already difficult authentication task impossible. Furthermore, of the some 1,200 pages of documentation only about 10% was allowed by the "owners of the information" to be shared by the Agency with Iran and the IAEA therefore requested these States to

agree to the Agency providing copies of the information to Iran. (Rauf and Kelley, 2015)

In 2007, ElBaradei was eager to solve the remaining issues including those of the "possible military dimension." Iran agreed. ElBaradei and Iran's chief negotiator Ali Larijani agreed on a work program. Issue by issue the outstanding problems were resolved. Centrifuge work, the HEU contamination, cylinders for fluorine gas, the polonium experiments, the mine-and-ore processing facility and the uranium metal document were all analyzed; new documents were put forth and the issues were closed. In November 2007, the first part of the work plan was completed. The remaining issues were likely to be resolved shortly.

According to Porter (2014:187) the US and its allies in the IAEA Board of Governors were not happy with this turn of things. The work plan was not to result in a "normalization" of the Iran file, rather the allies wanted a confession from Iran—an admission that it had secretly worked on a nuclear weapon. Under Secretary of State John Negroponte is quoted: "They have got to acknowledge that they had such a weapons program" (in Porter, 2014:188). The allies were in a hurry to get a resolution passed in the UN before the publication of the IAEA Director General's report on the issues. To the director it was underlined that the agency's credibility was at stake. Furthermore, the US even threatened budgetary consequences for the IAEA if ElBaradei continued to create obstacles to US diplomatic strategy in the Iranian nuclear program (ElBaradei, 2011:252–253).

The Final Assessment

On December 2, 2015 the IAEA published its final assessment on past and present outstanding issues regarding Iran's nuclear program. It concluded as before that no fissile material had been diverted to military uses but confirmed that Iran had an active nuclear program to develop a nuclear weapon until the end of 2003, in essence confirming the NIE 2007 estimate. While this activity was a coordinated effort, some activities did even take place until 2009: "These activities did not advance beyond feasibility and scientific studies and the acquisition of certain relevant technical competencies and capabilities" (IAEA, 2015:15).

After 2009, there are no indications of activities related to the development of a nuclear device. Some questions remained unresolved such as whether Iran had conducted tests on components of a nuclear explosive device. Iran claimed that work on detonators was aimed at improving the safety of conventional explosives. The IAEA did not find the explanations credible and concluded that the detonators had characteristics "relevant" to a nuclear explosive device.

The IAEA report not only confirms that Iran did have a nuclear weapons program before 2003, it also confirms the difficulty in establishing the existence of one in an unambiguous way, especially when the information originates from intelligence sources.

Rauf and Kelley (2015) published a critique of the IAEA final report the day of the IAEA Board meeting. According to them the process "has taken nearly a decade to reach a solution that easily could have been reached many years ago, had not ill advised politicization interfered with IAEA's technical work; and an incautious report in November 2011 based on dubious 'third party' or intelligence information and non-expert analysis."

They go through all the allegations in the "possible military dimension," look at the quality of the information and conclude:

> The IAEA cannot serve as a feedback loop to intelligence agencies on the veracity of information provided by them through safeguards inspections and assessments. Nor can or should the IAEA rely on such information without confirming its authenticity. This obviously leaves the IAEA in a difficult position as is clearly evidenced by the Iran PMD file where the Agency seems to have been caught short. (Rauf and Kelley, 2015:17)

Summarizing, Iran's nuclear activities have taken place in three stages: a coordinated nuclear program before 2003, limited activities of a scientific nature between 2003–2009 and a discontinuation of the activities since 2009. The IAEA report was a precondition for the implementation of the JCPOA, which started subsequently in January 16, 2016.

Iran's chief nuclear negotiator Abbas Araghchi is quoted as saying that the report "confirms that Iran's program was peaceful" (in Slavin, 2015). Critics of the Iran deal come, not surprisingly, to the conclusion that Iran had a "military dimension" and the word "possible" from the PMD may be removed (ACA, 2015).

Right before the publication of the IAEA report Iran's former President Rafsanjani stated in an interview that Iran considered acquiring a nuclear deterrent during the 1980–1988 Iran-Iraq war, as Iran feared that Saddam Hussein was close to developing nuclear bombs: "We were at war and we sought to have a possibility for the day the enemy might use a nuclear weapon. That was the thinking. But it never became real" (in Wilkin 2015).

Was Iran Treated Differently?

Have political concerns dominated the handling of the Iran file, and if so, how? Inspections are the basis of IAEA's mandate. Inspectors report what they find and the Director General reports to the Board of Governors on legal or technical non-compliance. The Board is not obliged to make a formal finding of non-compliance if it judges that circumstances do not warrant it. Political concerns play a role in the Board's decisions. Pierre Goldschmidt, a former director of the safeguards department, concludes: "there is a danger of setting bad precedents based on arbitrary criteria or judgments informed by political considerations" (Goldschmidt, 2009b:155).

Both ElBaradei (2011) and Goldschmidt (2009a) cite two examples of non-compliance, which, for political reasons, were not reported to the Security Council. South Korea began implementing the Additional Protocol in 2004. During the inspections, the IAEA found that experiments, not reported to the IAEA, had taken place with plutonium and enriched uranium. The South Korean government claimed it was unaware of the experiments and undertook corrective measures, including firing staff and creating a new oversight organization. South Korea was not reported to the Security Council due to US pressure. The board simply took note of the director's report.

In 2004, IAEA inspectors found that non-reported nuclear experiments had taken place in Egypt. The IAEA reported in February 2005 that Egypt had failed to declare 67 kg of imported UF4, 3 kg of uranium metal, 9.5 kg of imported thorium compounds, and unirradiated fuel rods containing 10 percent enriched U-235. Furthermore there was undeclared irradiation of uranium and thorium targets. Not only was Egypt not reported to the Security Council, Goldschmidt (2009a) assessed that the handling of the Egypt case put the credibility of the IAEA at stake.

A former E3 ambassador, on the board at the time, regrets today that South Korea was not reported.[4] As the Egypt case was similar, it could not be reported either. Political concerns intervene and countries are judged by different rules. Friends and allies are one thing, adversaries another. As ElBaradei notes: "But the Americans, especially in the case of Iran, insisted that the board was obliged to report to the Security Council every breach or violation" (ElBaradei, 2011:216).

There is also a question of proportionality. Iran was reported to the Security Council as a threat to world peace. At the same time a war was going on in Lebanon. A resolution on the war had been rejected in the Council. Secretary General Kofi Annan compared the two in terms of a threat to world peace: "This war in Lebanon was not considered a threat to international peace and security but the laboratory scale activity in Iran was" (ElBaradei, 2011:201).

Iran and North Korea, two countries that are often paired together, were also treated differently:

North Korea had walked out of the NPT and made explicit threats about developing nuclear weapons (and would in fact test its first weapons less than three months later, in October 2006), yet the Americans were ready to join them in a direct dialogue, and Chris Hill (Assistant US Secretary of State for East Asia and Pacific Affairs) seemed to be in Pyongyang every other day. By contrast Iran, which remained under safeguards and party to the NPT, was penalized for possibly having future intentions to develop nuclear weapons, and the Americans refused to talk to them without preconditions. (ElBaradei, 2011:203)

The legitimacy of the Security Council reporting has been questioned, not only by Iranians, but also by people in the West. Was it legitimate to report Iran to the Council in 2006, at a time when many of the reporting failures were corrected? Was it legitimate to make the suspension of enrichment Iran's legal obligation in relation to the inalienable right? Since the focus is on European views, I here quote six former European ambassadors to Tehran, who in 2011, published the following statement:

> In terms of international law, the position of Europe and the United States is perhaps less assured than is generally believed. Basically, it is embodied in a set of resolutions adopted by the UN Security Council authorizing the use of coercive measures in case of "threats to the peace." But what constitutes the threat? Is it the enrichment of uranium in Iranian centrifuges? ... In principle, however, nothing in international law or in the Nuclear Non-Proliferation Treaty forbids the enrichment of uranium. Besides Iran, several other countries, parties or not to the treaty, enrich uranium without being accused of "threatening the peace." And in Iran, this activity is submitted to international inspections by the International Atomic Energy Agency. These inspections, it is true, are constrained by a Safeguards Agreement dating from the 1970s. But it is also true that the IAEA has never uncovered in Iran any attempted diversion of nuclear material to military use.... Today, a majority of experts, even in Israel, seems to view Iran as striving to become a "threshold country," technically able to produce a nuclear weapon but abstaining from doing so for the present. Again, nothing in international law or the Nuclear Non-Proliferation Treaty prohibits such an ambition. Like Iran, several other countries are on their way to or have already reached such a threshold but have committed to not to acquire nuclear weapons. Nobody seems to bother them. (in Mousavian, 2012:228)[5]

Conclusions

With the knowledge we have today, what did Iran actually want to do? What were the objectives?

Iran, no doubt, aimed at becoming a threshold state, a state that had the capacity to build nuclear weapons. This is strategically a better position than actually having the weapons, which might invite military strikes and push non-nuclear neighboring countries to acquire weapons as well. Iran's neighbor, Iraq, did have a nuclear weapons program and Iran is surrounded by nuclear weapon states.

The Iranian government never made a decision to build weapons, not even during Ahmadinejad, as far as we know. Nevertheless, there have no doubt been groups in Iran who have supported the idea of becoming a nuclear weapon state. These interests are still there and the JCPOA implementation phase will imply a delicate balance between the political force supporting Iran's integration to the international community and those opposing it (Cronberg, 2016).

Why did Iran decide to discontinue its military nuclear program in 2003 and related activities in 2009?

The US military intervention in Iraq was, no doubt, the main factor in 2003. Iran was fearful of being the next in line for military intervention and clearly demonstrated the willingness to negotiate with the Americans. Regime change, the US policy at the time, was something to be avoided. The opportunity to negotiate with the Europeans, leading to the implementation of the Additional Protocol, no doubt reduced military ambitions. In 2009 there was the Green Movement; the country was in disarray. Sanctions had been approved by the Security Council and the existence of the facility at Fordow exposed.

Why did Iran continue its indigenous enrichment program after giving up on nuclear military intentions?

Firstly, to reject the suspension demanded by the P5+1 and made a legal requirement by the Security Council, illegitimate according to Iran, was an act of resistance, one built into the country's revolutionary ideology. It upheld the image of fighting the double standards of the West. There was also a legal basis, as enrichment was not prohibited. When Iran did suspend enrichment, it was underlined at every turn that this was voluntary and temporary.

Secondly, to accept suspension as a precondition before negotiations would have been a sign of weakness. In the eyes of its people Iran would give up something—to the enemy—without getting anything in return except negotiations with an uncertain outcome. It would be exchanging a "pearl with a lollipop."[6] Expanding the enrichment program was a way of building up bargaining power. This also worked. Iran continues to enrich with 5060 centrifuges spinning.

Thirdly, there is a complex web of prestige, scientific achievement and a quest for regional influence. Iran is a country of engineers and progress in science and technology is an organic part of the Supreme Leader's thinking. Access to nuclear technology, especially its most challenging part— enrichment—is a sign of scientific progress not immediately available to every state in the Middle East. Uranium enrichment became an object of national pride.

Finally, there was a real case of insecurity regarding the supply of fuel for the planned nuclear power program. Iran had been denied access to nuclear technology since the revolution. Even France, an earlier partner, declined to deliver fuel. Consequently, to enrich on Iranian soil was non-negotiable. The accept of the "fuel swap" by the Ahmadinejad government (both in the case of the Obama and the Turkey/Brazil agreement) was an illustrative case. Some enrichment to low grades in Iran was enough. The rest, to higher levels, could be done in Russia.

When judging Iran's nuclear intentions, the most important criteria, and one marginalized in the debates, is the fact that Iran has not withdrawn from the NPT. Had Iran had serious military intentions, the best option would have been to exit the NPT. There were proposals to leave the NPT in the parliament both in 2005–2006 due to reporting to the UNSC and in 2012–2013 due to the US/EU unilateral sanctions. No official withdrawal was ever initiated. Keeping countries like Iran in the NPT, on the right side of the nuclear border, strengthens the treaty and makes the world safer.

The fight for the right to enrich is a result of the intentional ambiguity of the NPT. This may have been functional in the early years. Today, when the world faces the expansion of nuclear technology, it is unacceptable. Furthermore, it weakens the treaty that two major actors in nonproliferation, the US and the EU, disagree in whether there is a right to enrich or not.

Notes

1 See General Hassan Firouzabadi on August 9, 2015. Available at http://theiranproject.com/blog/2015/08/09/iran-top-cmdr-supports-jcpoa-unsc-resolution/
2 Management solutions for such facilities have been proposed. For an overview and history of these arrangements see IAEA, 2015.
3 Of the 31 states that produce nuclear energy domestically, 11 have enrichment technology and five reprocess spent fuel.
4 Author's interview with a former E3 ambassador, December 18, 2015, South England.
5 The ambassadors were Richard Dalton (UK), Steen Hohwü-Christensen (S), Paul von Maltzahn (G), Guillaume Metten (Be), Francois Nicoullaud (Fr) and Robero Toscano (It).
6 Already in 2004 the head of state radio and TV Ali Larijani, who later become Ahmadinejads chief nuclear negotiator, was objected to the concessions Iran had given to the EU without getting anything in return. He commented that this was trading a "pearl with a lollipop". (Mousavian, 2012:189).

References

Acton, J. (2009) "The problem with nuclear mind reading," *Survival*, Vol. 51, No. 1, February-March, pp. 119–142.

Arms Control Association (ACA) (2015) The PMD Report: Reactions and Implications for the nuclear Deal with Iran. Available: www.armscontrol.org/events/2015-12-10/The-PMD-Report-Reactions-and-Implications-for-the-Nuclear-Deal-with-Iran [July 20, 2016]

Beeman, W. (2013) "Does Iran have the right to enrich uranium? The answer is yes," *The World Post*, 31 October. Available: www.huffingtonpost.com/william-o-beeman/does-iran-have-the-right-_b_4181347.html [September 8, 2016]

Cronberg, T. (2016) The great balancing act: EU policy choices during the implementation of the Iran deal, *EU Non-proliferation Paper No. 50*, Stockholm: SIPRI.

Dafna, L. (2004) "Nuclear disclosure on Iran unverified," *The Washington Post*, November 19. Available: www.washingtonpost.com/wp-dyn/articles/A61079-2004Nov18.html [July 20, 2016]

Davenport, K. and Philipp, E. (2016) 'A French view on the Iran deal: an interview with Ambassador Gérard Araud', *Arms Control Today*, July 5. Available: http://www.armscontrol.org/print/7550 [July 20, 2016]

Department of State (2005) *Adherence to and Compliance with Arms Control, Nonproliferation and Disarmament Agreements and Commitments*, August. Available: www.state.gov/documents/organization/52113.pdf [July 20, 2016]

ElBaradei, M. (2011) *The Age of Deception: Nuclear Diplomacy in Treacherous Times*, London: MacMillan.

Foster, W. (1968) In Conference of the Eighteen-Nation Committee on Disarmament, *Final Verbatim Record of the Three Hundred and Seventy-Eight Meeting*, Palais de Nation, Geneva, 13 March 1968 (ENDC/PV.376, para. 37). Available: https://archive.org/stream/4918260.0378.001.umich.edu#page/1/mode/2up [July 18, 2016]

Gates, R. (2014) *Memoirs of a Secretary at War*, New York: Alfred A. Knopf.

Goldschmidt, P. (2009a) "The IAEA reports on Egypt: reluctantly?" Available: http://carnegieendowment.org/2009/06/02/iaea-reports-on-egypt-reluctantly/1ztv [September 20, 2016]

Goldschmidt, P. (2009b) "Exposing nuclear non-compliance," *Survival*, Vol. 51, No. 1, pp. 143–164. Available: http://carnegieendowment.org/files/goldschmidt_survival20090201.pdf [July 20, 2016]

International Atomic Energy Agency (IAEA) (2003a) *Implementation of the NPT Safeguards Agreement in the Islamic Rebulic of Iran*, Board of Governors, IAEA GOV/2003/69, September 12. Available: https://www.iaea.org/sites/default/files/gov2003-69.pdf [July 20, 2016]

International Atomic Energy Agency (IAEA) (2003b) *Implementation of the NPT Safeguards Agreement in the Islamic Rebulic of Iran*, Board of Governors, IAEA GOV/2003/75, November 10. Available: www.iaea.org/sites/default/files/gov2003-75.pdf [July 20, 2016]

International Atomic Energy Agency (IAEA) (2005) *Multilateral Approaches to the Nuclear Fuel Cycle*. Expert Group Report submitted to the Director General of the International Atomic Energy Agency. INFCIRC/640, February 2.

International Atomic Energy Agency (IAEA) (2011) *Implementation of the NPT Safeguards Agreement and Relevant Provisions of Security Council Resolutions in the Islamic Republic of Iran*, Board of Governors, GOV/2011/65, November 8. Available: www.iaea.org/sites/default/files/gov2011-65.pdf [July 20, 2016]

International Atomic Energy Agency (IAEA) (2015) *Final Assessment on Past and Present Outstanding Issues Regarding Iran's Nuclear Programme*, Board of Governors, GOV/2015/68, December 2. Available: www.iaea.org/sites/default/files/gov-2015-68.pdf [July 20, 2016]

Joint Comprehensive Plan of Action (JCPOA) (2015), Vienna, July 14. Available: http://eeas.europa.eu/statements-eeas/docs/iran_agreement/iran_joint-comprehensive-plan-of-action_en.pdf [July 20, 2016]

Jonas, D. (2014) "Ambiguity defines the NPT: what does 'manufacture' mean?," *Loyola of Los Angeles International and Comparative Law Review*, pp. 262–280. Available: http://digitalcommons.lmu.edu/ilr/vol36/iss2/3 [September 3, 2016]

Joyner, D. (2011) "Iran's nuclear program and the legal mandate of the IAEA," *Jurist*, 9 November. Available: http://jurist.org/forum/2011/11/dan-joyner-iaea-report.php [July 20, 2016]

Kerr, P. (2016) *Iran's Nuclear Program: Tehran's Compliance with International Obligations*, Washington, DC: Congressional Research Service.

Mousavian, S. (2012) *The Iranian Nuclear Crisis: A Memoir*. Washington, DC: Carnegie Endowment for International Peace.

National Intelligence Estimate (NIE) (2007) *Iran: Nuclear Intentions and Capabilities*. Washington: National Intelligence Council. Available: http://www.dni.gov/files/documents/Newsroom/Reports%20and%20Pubs/20071203_release.pdf [July 20, 2016]

Porter, G. (2014) *Manufactured Crisis: The Untold Story of the Iran Nuclear Scare*, Charlottesville: Just World Books.

Rauf, T. and Kelley R. (2015) "Assessing the IAEA 'assessment' of 'possible military dimensions' of Iran's nuclear program," *Atomic Reporters*. Available: http://www.atomicreporters.com/2015/12/assessing-the-iaea-assessment-of-possible-military-dimensions-of-irans-nuclear-programme/ [July 20, 2016]

Rosecrance, R. (1968) After NPT, What? Department of State. Policy Planning Council, Resources from the National Security Archives Nuclear Documentation Project. Available: http://nsarchive.gwu.edu/nukevault/ebb253/doc27.pdf [July 20, 2016]

Senate Select Committee on Intelligence Hearing (2012) *Statement for the Record by Director of National Intelligence James R. Clapper – Worldwide Threat Assessment of the United States Intelligence Community*, 31 January. Available: www.dni.gov/files/documents/Newsroom/Testimonies/20120131_testimony_ata.pdf [July 20, 2016]

Slavin, B. (2015) "New report confirms Iran's nuclear weapons program," *AlMonitor*, December 2. Available: www.al-monitor.com/pulse/originals/2015/12/iaea-iran-report-nuclear-weapons-program.html [July 20, 2016]

Spector, L. (1995) Repentant Nuclear Proliferants, in Evan, W. and Nanda, V. (eds.), *Nuclear Proliferation and the Legality of Nuclear Weapons*, Lanham: University Press of America, pp. 23–24

Tirone, J. (2014) "Iran nuclear past said not impediment to ending standoff," *Bloomberg Business*, November 4. Available: www.bloomberg.com/news/articles/2014-11-04/iran-nuclear-past-said-not-impediment-to-ending-standoff [July 20, 2016]

Treaty on the Non-Proliferation of Nuclear Weapons (NPT) (1968), Article IV. Available: http://www.un.org/en/conf/npt/2005/npttreaty.html [July 20, 2016]

Wilkin, S. (2015) "Iran considered nuclear weapons during 1980s Iraq war, ex-president says," *Reuters*, October 29. Available: www.reuters.com/article/us-iran-nuclear-rafsanjani-idUSKCN0SN0E720151029 [September 8, 2016]

Zhang, X. (2006) "The riddle of 'inalienable right' in Article IV of the Treaty on the Non-Proliferation of Nuclear Weapons: intentional ambiguity," *Chinese Journal of International Law*, Vol. 5, pp. 647–662.

5   The Power of Sanctions

The objective of sanctions is to change a country's behavior. In the Iran case, the goal was to coerce Iran into renouncing its possible interest in nuclear weapons and, as an indication of this, to suspend uranium enrichment. In spite of "crippling" sanctions, enrichment continued. Iran increased the number of its centrifuges and, along with these scientific achievements, the level and intensity of Iranian pride and even nuclear nationalism grew, too. Nevertheless, the sanctions did have an impact on the negotiations and helped create conditions for the final deal.

This chapter looks at the effect of the sanctions regime and the early process of technology denial. It identifies some of the economic and humanitarian consequences in Iran as well as Iran's strategies to cope with them. Although the deal has been in effect for less than a year (at the time of writing), the contours of future conflicts related to sanctions relief are already visible. These imply a great balancing act involving not only the political forces inside Iran but also those in the US. In this conflict zone, Europe has an important role to play.

What Do Sanctions Do?

> Economic disruption caused by sanctions is expected to translate into political pressure that will eventually compel the leadership in the target country to change its policies, or will lead to its overthrow. (Portela, 2010:3)

The relationship between economic pain and policy changes is by no means automatic. Galtung (1967) talks about a "societal transmission belt" in order to explain the link between economic pain and the impact of sanctions. Instead of compelling changes in the government's behavior—or instigating its disintegration—the population may get used to living under the economic burden. Furthermore, the leaders may use sanctions to create an image of the enemy, thereby rallying the people "behind the flag" against them.

President Ahmadinejad succeeded in defining the nuclear program as an object of national pride, creating the conditions for "nuclear nationalism" (Borhani, 2014). Consequently, one of the central questions of sanctions theory is how "economic distress galvanizes political change in the target country" (Portela 2010:5).

In nonproliferation, sanctions are a more coercive tool than inspections, but less coercive than military threats and interventions. They are economic warfare and operate in the same way as military warfare: by inflicting pain and offering continued suffering unless the target complies (Schelling, 1966). The European Union increasingly uses sanctions in its foreign policy. But "sanctions cannot be used alone and never without a strategy," according to a high-level EU official responsible for EU sanctions.[1] "And never," according to the Swedish Foreign Minister Carl Bildt (2013) "are they a replacement for a strategy."

There are two types of sanctions: targeted sanctions and more general economic sanctions. Targeted sanctions "focus their impact on leaders, political elites and segments of society believed responsible for objectionable behavior, while reducing collateral damage to the general population and third countries" (Hufbauer and Oegg 2000:3). Since the 1990s, the EU has focused on targeted sanctions in an effort to avoid large-scale humanitarian impacts on the population. "We must avoid sanctions that harm the wider population," EU Commissioner Ferrero-Waldner noted in a statement, indicating further: "We work with civil society groups, parliamentarians, government officials and others to foster as broad a basis as possible for democratic practice- changing mind-sets, not regimes" (Ferrero-Waldner, 2006).

The most common practice of the EU is to adopt sanctions called for by UN Security Council resolutions. In the absence of these, the EU may impose sanctions of its own, often called unilateral, in contrast to UN sanctions, which are universally binding. Both the 2003 European Security Strategy and the WMD Strategy foresaw the use of sanctions as an instrument of security policy. The sanctions on Iran's nuclear program were the first such usage of sanctions as envisioned by these EU documents. US sanctions on Iran differed radically from the EU sanctions; the former constituted a seamless web of restrictions since 1979 related not only to the nuclear program, but also to state-sponsored terrorism and human rights (Cordesman et al., 2013; Katzman, 2016).

Early Technology Denial

The 1979 Islamic Revolution brought Iran's nuclear program to a halt. After an electricity shortage in 1981, the Islamic government determined to complete the Bushehr nuclear power plant—at the time only 80 percent constructed—still a far cry from the twenty plants envisioned under the Shah.

The Atomic Energy Organization of Iran asked IAEA Director General Hans Blix to provide technical assistance for fuel production and uranium conversion and to cooperate with corresponding Iranian research institutions.

Iran's plan was to run the Bushehr reactor with enriched uranium provided by Western firms. The first choice was Eurodif, a French joint venture with Iran as a partner. Eurodif refused to sell fuel to Iran. The US declared that it would deny Iran any nuclear technology and had persuaded France to refuse reactor fuel for Bushehr. The US argument was that Iran had sufficient oil and gas reserves for power generation. Nuclear reactors were expensive, unnecessary and could be used for military purposes. The Ronald Reagan administration intervened and blocked any nuclear assistance to Iran. Also, the IAEA abandoned its agreement. The US convinced key European allies to use stricter criteria on technology transfer than those used by the IAEA.

In late 1990, President George H.W. Bush called a meeting of the Nuclear Suppliers Group (NSG) to discuss even tougher guidelines for "problem NPT states," focusing especially on Iran. The US called on members to agree on a separate regime for Iran consisting of a complete ban on all trade in nuclear technology and material. The US policy of denial was completely transparent. Assistant Secretary of State Edward Djerejian told a House subcommittee in 1991: "The US engages in no nuclear cooperation with Iran, and we have urged other nuclear suppliers, including China, to adopt a similar policy" and further "We have been in touch with a number of potential nuclear suppliers (to warn) that engaging in any form of nuclear cooperation, whether under safeguards or not, is highly imprudent" (in Kempster, 1991).

At this time there were no suspicions on military intentions; the need for fuel and technology was for an unfinished nuclear power plant. Denying cooperation was a clear violation of NPT Article IV, which in addition to the inalienable right states: "All the Parties to the Treaty undertake to facilitate, and have the right to participate in, the fullest possible exchange of equipment, materials and scientific and technological information for the peaceful uses of nuclear energy" (NPT, 1968). The French protested but complied. French nuclear scientist Pierre Villaros, visiting Iran as a member of an IAEA delegation in 1993, deplored the fact that Iran was under de facto embargo on nuclear equipment (van England, 1993).

In the late 1980s, the only source of technology and know-how to which Iran had access was the covert proliferation network of the Pakistani scientist, A.Q. Khan, which sold centrifuge designs and plans for a complete enrichment plant. The Khan network also supplied technologies related to military applications, but there is no evidence that the Iranians bought anything related to military applications. The clandestine efforts to access nuclear technology can, at least in the early phases of the Iranian search for nuclear solutions, be explained by the denial policies of the US and the NSG to which the Germany, France and the IAEA submitted.

Additional secrecy is explained by Iran's contacts with China. China was also under US pressure not to cooperate with Iran. China had, however, supplied Iran test reactors and uranium. The agreement was not made public because the US-China Nuclear Cooperation Agreement was to be signed and submitted to Congress in 1985 (Holt and Nikitin, 2015).

"Sanctions Is What We Do"

Nuclear technology denial was only part of the complex web of sanctions levied by the US on Iran after the revolution. This included also a complete trade ban, banking prohibitions, refusal of all aid to Iran (also through international institutions), targeting individuals and entities and freezing Iran's assets in the US. When I visited the Iran desk at the US State Department in 2012 to discuss sanctions, the comment was: "sanctions is what we do." In spite of the US sanctions, the reporting of Iran to the Security Council introduced a new, tougher sanctions era, crippling the economy.

Below is an overview of the UN universal sanctions on Iran and the EU and US nuclear-related unilateral sanctions. This is not a detailed account, as my interest is not to go in detail but rather to understand how the P5+1 have dealt with the sanctions and how the Iranians have responded. For a more comprehensive account see Cordesman et al. (2013) and Katzman (2016).

UN Universal Sanctions (2006–2010)

In the four-year period of 2006–2010, the UNSC approved four sanctions resolutions on Iran. UN resolution 1737 imposed a worldwide freeze on the assets and properties of listed nuclear entities. The list was expanded in subsequent resolutions. Resolution 1747 banned Iranian arms exports and requested that international financial institutions and states refrain from making grants or loans to Iran (other than for development and humanitarian purposes). Resolutions 1803 and 1929 authorized the inspection of cargo where export of banned goods was suspected. Resolution 1929 also banned activities related to ballistic missiles capable of delivering a nuclear weapon and required UNSC approval to sell arms to Iran. Investments by Iran abroad in uranium mining and related nuclear technologies were also prohibited. The resolutions taken together also ban the export of most dual-use items to Iran as well as travel of specific Iranians.

The UN sanctions did not at any time ban civilian trade or investments in Iran. However, resolution 1929 links the revenues from Iran's oil sector to its funding of sensitive nuclear activities. This resolution is interpreted as UN support to countries that ban their companies' activities with Iran's oil sector (Katzman, 2016:50).

These sanctions are now lifted in UN Security Council resolution 2231 of July 20, 2015. The sanctions remaining are an arms embargo for a maximum of five years (subject to UNSC approval) and a call not to launch ballistic missiles designed to carry a nuclear weapon (for a maximum of eight years). The resolution also requires Iran to submit to the Joint Commission applications to purchase dual-use items.

An innovation is the "snap-back" function included in resolution 2231. Any signatory of the Iran deal may report an issue of non-compliance to the Security Council, when no agreement is reached via a conflict resolution mechanism of the Joint Commission. Within 30 days, the Council must decide, according to paragraph 11, "to continue in effect the terminations" of earlier sanctions. If one permanent member of the Security Council votes against a draft resolution for the termination not to continue, all the sanctions will "snap back." Sanctions terminated may thus be re-imposed by one of the P5 members, even if all the other 14 members would be against.

The EU and US Unilateral Sanctions (2010–2012)

In 2010–2012, there was a coordinated effort from the US and the EU to approve unilateral (as opposed to UN universal) sanctions on Iran. The US pressured the Europeans to join the Obama policy of "crippling" sanctions after the Iranians ignored the president's gestures to an opening. Obtaining European agreement was not easy. The French were already advocating for tougher sanctions but the Germans were critical. An oil embargo meant additional economic pain for the Southern European economies already suffering under the Eurocrisis. Both Sweden and Finland were skeptical but consented in the name of consensus. Reportedly, the argument that ultimately convinced the Europeans was that such sanctions were a clear message to Israel not to attack (see the next chapter for the military option).

The most effective instrument of the sanctions regime was to exclude Iran from the banking and financial systems. Already in 2006, the US Treasury Department had worked to persuade foreign banks to cease their dealings with Iran. The Department made overtures to 145 banks in 60 countries. The argument was that Iran was using the international financial system to fund terrorist groups and acquire weapons-related technology (Katzman, 2016:28). Fines and forfeiture of assets were imposed on those helping Iran to access the financial system and on foreign banks that conducted transactions with sanctioned Iranian banks.

The EU froze Iran Central Bank assets in January 2012 and in October banned all transactions with Iranian banks unless authorized. The financial system, SWIFT, expelled Iranian banks from the electronic payment transfer system. Both the US and the EU denied foreign aid and grants to Iran. Like the US, which had banned all transactions with Iran's oil and gas sector, the EU now banned all dealings with Iran's energy sector. Moreover, financing companies involved in the Iranian energy sector were prohibited.

Following the UN resolutions, both the EU and the US banned weapon exports to Iran, including ballistic-missile technology as well as dual-use items. Both sanctioned designated entities that dealt with the nuclear issue; the EU also froze their assets. Like the US earlier, the EU banned Iran Air Cargo—the freight division of the national airline—from access to airports, froze shipping assets, and prohibited insurance and reinsurance for Iranian firms. By the start of 2013, the US and the EU had a comprehensive set of sanctions in place prohibiting financial transactions in general and involvement in the Iranian oil and gas sector.

By implementation day (January 16, 2016) the EU had lifted almost all of the sanctions, though some EU sanctions targeting special entities such as the IRGC remained. Most of the US sanctions remained, as they were not "nuclear-related." The JCPOA opened up some trade between Iran and the US (passenger aircraft and luxury goods). The UN-defined arms embargo and restrictions on ballistic missile technology remained both for the US and the EU.

What Did the Sanctions Do?

At the height of the sanctions regime, in 2013 and before the deal, there were a number of pessimistic analyses on what the sanctions regime could or had achieved (ICG, 2013; Khajepour, Marashi and Parsi, 2013; Blockmans and Waizer, 2013). All authors agreed that sanctions had not succeeded in advancing the ultimate objective of transforming Iranian foreign and security policy. They agree that Iran is resistant to economic pressures and that this increases the domestic power of the hardliners. The ICG's study refers to two opposite perspectives: the West viewed sanctions as coercive instruments to pressure Iran to curtail its nuclear activities; Iran, in turn, perceived sanctions as a thinly disguised pretext to undermine the regime. The NIAC study by Khajepour et al. focusing on the Iranian narrative portrays the Western powers as a brutal, immoral group of governments, whose core interest is to keep Iran underdeveloped and dependent. Iran, while suffering economically, continued to gain respect from developing countries. Furthermore, the authors foresaw a time will come when the Europeans will not blindly support the US strategy and will take a different path: "As long as Iran stands firm, global sanctions fatigue—including in Europe—will ultimately cause the collapse of this policy" (2013:16). In retrospect, after the JCPOA, what did the sanctions achieve?

The Economic Impact

Iran's economic losses due to the US and EU sanctions were indeed "crippling," to use the term of art. In 2010–13, Iran's crude oil exports fell from 2.5 million barrels per day (B/D) in 2011 to about 1.1 million B/D. The economy shrank by 9 percent in two years ending March 2014. Iran's ability to procure equipment for its nuclear and missile development as well as to import conventional weapons were constricted. The value of the *rial* declined 56 percent from January 2012 to 2014 and the estimated actual inflation rate was between 50 and 70 percent. In 2011–13, industrial production fell by 60 percent (Katzman, 2016).

In addition to these macroeconomic indicators, the structure of the economy changed. Sanctions created a shadow economy. As a senior Iranian official remarked, "after living under sanctions for three decades, we are now in a position to open up a consultancy and share our know-how with other countries facing similar situation" (ICG, 2013:16). Front companies, middlemen, smuggling networks and re-exporting of Western goods through Turkey as well as tricks to hide the origin of product are all part of the resilience of the Iranian grey economy, the structures of which will be hard to dismantle. This shadow economy reportedly accounted for 21 percent of the GDP (ICG, 2013:37). The actors of this shadow economy are, illustratively, being called the "merchants of sanctions." These merchants of sanctions, not only located in Iran but also in the United Arab Emirates, China and Europe, are obviously not supportive of the final deal.

The Impact on the Population

Although the impact on the population was not a primary goal but rather an unintended consequence, the sanctions' "societal transmission belt" affected the lives of ordinary citizens. This impact was uneven. Those that suffered the least are the rich and the poor (Katzman, 2016). The elites maintained access to luxury goods in Tehran and many, especially those in the IRGC and the "merchants of sanctions," became extremely wealthy. The poor did not suffer proportionally as much—thanks to state aid programs—but the number of people living under the poverty line increased. A particularly vulnerable group were the three million Afghan refugees, especially women and children.

The middle class, the source for societal reform, was decimated. Other victims include democracy and the rule of law. A report by the International Civil Society Action Network (ICAN, 2012) documents how sanctions destroyed the sources of societal change in Iran. Many civil society organizations and charities that survive on voluntary activism could not survive when people retreated from voluntary work. Instead, former volunteers found themselves working longer hours and often at multiple jobs to meet their economic needs. With private enterprise in demise, more people became dependent on the state and thus fearful of engaging in civil activism. Limitations placed on the transfer of funds, including foreign, endangered the work of civil society organizations, and many of these organizations ceased their activities (ICAN, 2012).

The report further underscores that women bore the brunt of the distress. When jobs are scarce, conservative values push women out of the labor market and into the domestic sphere. When families cannot support their children, girls do not go to school and the rate of child marriages increases. A new phenomenon of "street women" arises, unknown in Muslim countries.

The most difficult problem for the population was access to medicine, particularly specialized medicine. Although medical items were exempt from sanctions, the banks of pharmaceutical companies were fearful of potential fines and chose not to have transactions with Iran. When the European Parliamentary delegation visited Iran in December 2013, we met with all the UN representatives in Tehran to discuss the situation. In a memo to us, the United Nations Children's Fund (UNICEF) representative underlined the serious problem with specialized medicine, reporting that, each year, 5–7.5 million Iranians fell below the poverty line, due to treatment expenses. UNICEF had problems acquiring vaccines, which were mediated to them through banks in Tajikistan.[2] The UNICEF Iran office was completely cut off from support of European donors, which significantly affected their ability to support social programs for the most vulnerable groups.

Airline safety suffered from sanctions. Since the US trade ban in 1995, 1,700 passengers and crew have been killed in air accidents, although, as Katzman (2016:67) points out, it is not clear how many of these accidents were due to lack of US spare parts. Air pollution affected health. Unable to import gasoline, Iran produced gasoline using inappropriate methods, resulting in more impurities and increased pollution. This forced authorities to limit car driving and even to temporarily close schools. During the Iranian year ending March 12, 2013, there were an estimated 4,460 deaths from air pollution.[3] The World Bank, succumbing to US pressure, ceased to provide environmental financing to Iran to combat these environmental hazards.

Iranian Strategies for Coping

Iran's response was not only to increase non-oil exports and substitute imports by domestic production. The ideological answer was the "resistance economy," articulated in a 24-article plan introduced by Supreme Leader Khamenei in February 2014 following a ban on benzene exports to Iran. The resistance economy is an indigenous and scientific economic model that projects an Islamic and revolutionary culture.[4] It is about reduced imports, increased exports, economic growth and social welfare. Capital markets exist but should be coordinated. Consumers are important and a change in their habits is critical for the new (resistance) economic structures.

The core dimensions are "indigenous" and "scientific." In the Supreme Leader's view, mastering science and technology leads to self-reliance, which is a precondition for political independence. He has interpreted technology denial by the West not only as effort to prevent Iran from developing a nuclear weapon, but also as obstruction of scientific progress in Iran:

> It is hard for the global arrogance to accept that the talented Iranian nation has been able to take great strides in the field of science and technology, especially in the field of nuclear technology. They want Iran's energy to be always dependent on oil, since oil is vulnerable to the policies of world powers. They aim to control other nations with invisible ropes. (in Sadjadpour, 2008:23)

The nuclear program has come to embody Iran's vision for its future: the quest for influence in the region, resistance to superpowers and their intervention, the mastery of advanced technology and indigenous research and development. The nationalistic sentiments attached to the nuclear program are not only shared by the political elite, both the hardliners and the reformists, but also by the general population.

In a survey of public opinion conducted by Tehran University in cooperation with the University of Maryland following JPOA in 2013, strong majorities rejected the idea that Iran's nuclear research activities should be limited or that Iran should halve the number of centrifuges spinning. At the same time, the majority of the respondents were willing to cap the enrichment to 5 percent and to support an agreement with a strict control regime (Newsom, 2014).

The Grey Zone of Interpretations

Less than a year into the JCPOA implementation, sanction-related conflicts are brewing. Some of these are the effect of remaining US sanctions, others to different interpretations of the JCPOA and UN Security Council

Resolution 2231. Fear of potential penalties has lead to overcompliance by European banks. One of the more contentious issues is the "U-turn."

In November 2008, the Department of the Treasury prohibited US banks from handling any indirect dollar transactions with Iranian banks (although no dollars exchange hands, trade deals at some point are transferred in dollars). This restriction was never meant to be lifted (Katzman, 2016). The Treasury Secretary has suggested "that the US 'might' take steps to license transactions by foreign (non-Iranian) clearinghouses to acquire dollars that might facilitate transactions with Iran, without providing Iran with dollars directly" (Bauer, 2016).

Banks in Europe fear they will be fined and possibly cut off from the US financial market if they re-enter Iran. Due to risks of terrorist financing and money laundering, indirect dollar transactions in commercial relations with Iran could be viewed as a "serious threat [...] to the integrity of the international financing system" (FATF, 2016). The Iranians, in turn, argue that this restriction is in conflict with the JCPOA, which obligates the US to remove all restrictions that prevent Iran from obtaining the full benefits of sanctions relief (JCPOA, 2015:24).

The US secondary sanctions targeting foreign firms doing business with Iran are lifted but with "non-nuclear" exceptions. Both the EU and the US still maintain sanctions on some parts of the IRGC and affiliated entities. As the IRGC is seamlessly integrated in the Iranian economy, it is difficult to distinguish when there is IRGC involvement.

In August 2015, Adam Szubin, the US Treasury's Acting Under Secretary for Terrorism and Financial Intelligence, stated in written testimony to the Senate Banking Committee: "A foreign bank that conducts or facilitates a significant financial transaction with Iran's Mahan Air, the IRGC-controlled construction firm Khatam al-Anbiya, or Bank Saderat will risk losing its access to the U.S. financial system, and this is not affected by the nuclear deal" (in Dehghanpisheh and Torbati, 2015).

Khatam al-Anbiya, controlled by the IRGC, is Iran's largest contractor and engineering firm, with hundreds of registered companies doing business with hundreds of contractors. The company is active in most construction including dams, water diversion systems, highways, tunnels, buildings, heavy-duty structures, three-dimensional trusses, offshore construction, water supply systems and water, gas and oil main pipelines. European companies involved in infrastructure projects will no doubt come in contact with this engineering conglomerate. Will they risk being shut out of the US financial structures?

Sanctions as Strategic Competition

Sanctions are meant to be a coercive tool to change a country's behavior. This tool also impacts world markets. The unilateral EU sanctions reduced Iranian exports to the EU by 86 percent and EU imports by 26 percent in 2012–13. The decline was dramatic, and European businesses have eagerly waited for the lifting of sanctions in order to re-enter the Iranian market. The German Chamber of Commerce is expecting German exports to Iran to double to 5 billion euro in three years and reach 10 billion in five years. Italy is also expecting economic growth from Iranian markets. Italy's exports plummeted from 7 billion euro to 1.2 after 2012.[5] The Europeans are ready to re-enter the Iranian market, even if remaining US sanctions pose restrictions.

Years of sanctions have reduced the US-Iran trade to a minimal level. Yet in 2011, when the EU agreed to coordinate unilateral sanctions with the United States, US exports to Iran climbed 35 percent while European combined exports dropped 77 percent, the cause for much frustration.[6] US companies could receive waivers that were not available for non-US companies. European officials refer to US "double standards." The JCPOA, however, opens up some US trade. Airplanes and parts as well as luxury goods (carpets, caviar and nuts) are exempt from sanctions. Boeing has already sold 100 airplanes but the Republican-led House of Representatives approved measures to block the sales. Airbus in Europe has also sold 114 planes to Iran. Boeing Vice-Chairman Ray Conner argued that if Boeing is not allowed to sell the planes, neither should Airbus. Airbus planes also include parts made in the US, making them subject to US legislation banning sales of planes to Iran. In October 2016 the US government granted both Airbus and Boeing permission to sell aircraft to Iran (Gambrell, 2016).

A trade war is under way. US regulators can effectively block European advances on the Iranian market. Surprisingly enough, a US economist following Iran indicated that while "the Iranian market was big, it was not that big," indicating that the US could refrain from entering the Iranian market. When discussing the complex picture of US sanctions still in force, she commented that, in the future, the European companies will have to decide whether they want to work with the US or with Iran. In the latter case, they should be prepared to employ a lot of sanction lawyers.[7]

How have the sanctions affected the other partners, Russia and China? Russia became the leading supplier of technology and equipment to Iran in the 1990s, providing fighter jets, missile systems, submarines and armored vehicles. This trade has been radically reduced, not only because of UN sanctions, but also due to US and EU banking restrictions. Trade between the two countries was reduced by 40 percent in 2012. Today, while Russia sees some openings, the talk is about a "cautious partnership" (RIAC

2014:19, 39). The risk of losing Western contracts or, worse still, access to Western financial markets restrain Russian companies from working in Iran:

> Russian businesses, especially those associated with international business and therefore affected by international (primarily American) sanctions are naturally not willing to scrap their beneficial ties with Western partners in exchange for an unclear future in Iran. Lukoil, which has a large business in the United States has opted out of fostering business ties with Iran, despite promising developments in the oil sector. (RIAC 2014:28)

Iran's Russian partners are in no hurry to invest in Iran. One reason is "that Iran has turned into a no-man's land that is unattractive for business and threatens the international reputation of those who choose to do business there" (RIAC 2014:20). On the other hand, Russia fears that, in the JCPOA era, political reformers in Iran will be oriented toward the West. Consequently, Russia is struggling to determine how to win—or at least not lose—the fight for Iran. The answer is the nuclear sector, as Russia already has a platform in Bushehr. Another answer is military technology and weapons export (subject to UN approval).[8]

China is the main buyer of Iranian oil and sees its imports as legitimate. China agreed to UNSC Resolution 1929 after key exemptions were added to allow for continued foreign investments in Iran's energy sector (Cordesman et. al., 2013). Nevertheless, China reduced its oil imports from Iran and sought other supply sources from Saudi Arabia and Iraq. Although China's investments in Iran's infrastructure are still high, those in the Iranian oil sector have decreased. Today the Iranian-Sino relationship is unbalanced: Iran is much more dependent on China than vice versa.

China will be a major competitor in the JCPOA era, not only to Russia but also to Europe. European products, particularly consumer products, may have a competitive advantage in quality. When the European parliament delegation visited President Rouhani's chief-of-staff, the well-known economist Mohammad Nahavandian in December 2013, he commented that trade with China was a "forced choice" during the sanctions. The Iranians would much prefer the higher-quality European products. Whether this still hold true after sanctions relief remains to be seen.

Conclusions

In 2013, why did the Iranians return to the negotiation table and agree to the interim JPOA that November? It would be tempting to conclude that US sanctions depleted the Iranians of influence and that European sanctions surprised the Iranian decision-makers and compelled them to the table.

Yet such a conclusion does not acknowledge that the Supreme Leader already agreed in 2011 to negotiate with the Americans, and that in November 2013, the JPOA was agreed after secret meetings in Oman. The final deal is a result of the political will of the two presidents. Without the persistence of the presidents, the US and Iran would not have been able to close a deal, sanctions or no. Sanctions did contribute to the necessary conditions, as the economy and sanctions relief became an issue in the Iranian presidential elections. The population drew its own conclusion and voted for Rouhani, a sign that the "societal transmission belt" for the sanction had worked.

In the sanctions regime, two measures rise above others as especially effective. Firstly, the European sanctions that cut Iranian access to financial structures (SWIFT) were crucial. Trade volumes were reduced radically during and after 2012 when these sanctions entered into force. Secondly, the economic impact of the sanctions was reinforced by psychological factors related to the reputation of companies dealing with Iran. This understanding successfully permeated not only companies in the West but also in Russia and China. In this respect, the outcome represents "effective multilateralism," although reluctant and involuntary for these two countries.

Sanctions, during the Iran process, have created a phenomenon of "overcompliance." The remaining US sanctions, possible penalties and the threat of being closed off from the US financial market creates fear. This fear lingers in European banks today. Insecurity persists due to the complex US legislative system dealing with money laundering, dollar transactions, terrorism financing and the like, as well as risks related to possible new sanctions. Clear instructions are needed, but obviously very difficult to provide.

Sanctions on Iran, including the early technology denial policies, cut Iranian access to nuclear and military technology. Access to dual-use technologies was and will continue to be restricted. Under the JCPOA, there is a special procurement channel of the Joint Commission charged with monitoring Iran's access to these technologies. Given Iran's focus on science and technology and its belief that the West uses technology restrictions to prevent economic progress in Iran, technology access will remain a sensitive issue and a JCPOA vulnerability during the implementation phase.

European targeted sanctions were meant to avoid hardship for ordinary citizens. Still, sanctions had dramatic consequences for the population, particularly women and children, although there were only minor public demonstrations. Long-term consequences for civil society, democracy and the rule of law in Iran raise the question of the legitimacy of sanctions, even if targeted. The sanctions have largely been ineffective in relation to the elites and the decision-makers and "effective" in terms of affecting the population at large.

Notes

1 Author's interview with a senior EEAS sanctions' official, December 2015, London.
2 Information from a memo handed to the European Parliament's delegation at meeting with UN representatives, Tehran in December 2013.
3 Information from the above and discussions at the meeting.
4 For a translation of the Supreme Leader's speech introducing the resistance economy, see "Iran document: Supreme Leader's plan for "resistance economy,"", EA Worldview, March 5, 2014, http://eaworldview.com/2014/03/iran-document-supreme-leaders-plan-resistance-economy/.
5 This economic information is available at: www.dw.com/en/german-industry-eyes-iran-as-sanctions-lift/a-18986738 and http://www.thelocal.it/20160125/italy-looks-to-iran-to-revive-trade
6 This information comes from an email by Jonathan Tirone of June 4, 2014 forwarded by the European Parliamentary Research Service (Jan Baeverstroem) to the parliament's Iran delegation.
7 Author's interview with an economist specializing on Iran, February 18, 2015. Washington, DC.
8 Author's interview with an economist specializing on Iran, October 2, 2015. Moscow.

References

Bauer, K. (2016) *Potential U.S. Clarification of Financial Sanctions Regulation.* April 5. Available: www.washingtoninstitute.org/policy-analysis/view/potential-u.s.-clarification-of-financial-sanctions-regulations [October 8, 2016]
Bildt, C. (2013) Speech given at the Carnegie Nuclear Policy Conference. April 10, Washington DC.
Blockmans, S. and Waizer, S. (2013) *E3+3 Coercive Diplomacy towards Iran: Do the Economic Sanctions Add Up?* CEPS Policy Brief, No. 292, June 6. Brussels.
Borhani, M. (2014). *Understanding the Nuclear Motivations of the Islamic Republic of Iran: New Approach.* Unpublished thesis dated August 27, 2014.
Cordesman, A., Gold, B., Khazai S. and Bosserman, B. (2013) *U.S and Iranian Strategic Competition: Sanctions, Energy, Arms Control, and Regime Change,* April 19, New York: Center for Strategic and International Studies.
Dehghanpisheh, B. and Torbati, Y. (2015) "Firms linked to Revolutionary Guards to win sanctions relief under Iran deal," *Reuters,* August 9. Available: www.reuters.com/article/us-iran-nuclear-sanctions-idUSKCN0QE08320150809 [September 6, 2016]
Ferrero-Waldner, B. (2006) *European Strategies for Promoting Democracy in Post-Communist Countries,* International Conference, Institute for Human Sciences, Vienna, January 20.
Financial Action Task Force (FATF) (2016) *FATF Public Statement,* February 19. Available: www.fatf-gafi.org/publications/high-riskandnon-cooperativejurisdictions/documents/public-statement-february-2016.html [September 7, 2016]
Galtung, J. (1967) "On the effects of international economic sanctions, with examples from the case of Rhodesia," *World Politics,* No. 19, pp. 378–416.

Gambrell, J. (2016) "US grants Airbus, Boeing a Chance to sell airplanes to Iran," *Bloomberg*, September 21 [Online]. Available: www.bloomberg.com/news/articles/2016-09-21/urgent-airbus-says-us-grants-license-for-planes-in-iran-deal [October 4, 2016]

Holt, M. and Nikitin M. B. D. (2015) *U.S.-China Nuclear Cooperation Agreement.* Washington D. C.: Congressional Research Center.

Hufbauer, G. and Oegg, B. (2000) "Targeted sanctions: a policy alternative?" Paper submitted to the symposium *Sanctions Reform? Evaluating the Economic Weapon in Asia and the World*, February 23. Washington: Institute for International Economics, pp. 11–21.

International Civil Society Action Network (ICAN) (2012) *Killing Them Softly: The Stark Impact of Sanctions on the Lives of Ordinary Iranians*, Brief 3, July 2012. Available: www.icanpeacework.org/wp-content/uploads/2013/04/WWS-Iran-Killing-Them-Softly-2013-Edit.pdf [July 20, 2016]

International Crisis Group (2013) *Spider Web: The Making and Unmaking of Iran Sanctions*. February 25. Report No. 138, Brussels.

Joint Comprehensive Plan of Action (JCPOA) (2015) Vienna, July 14. Available: http://eeas.europa.eu/statements-eeas/docs/iran_agreement/iran_joint-comprehensive-plan-of-action_en.pdf [July 16, 2016]

Katzman, K. (2016) *Iran Sanctions*, CRS Report, June 17.

Kempster, N. (1991) "U.S. calls for nuclear embargo against Iran: Mideast: A House panel is told that Washington believes Tehran is trying to develop weapons," *Los Angeles Times*, November 21.

Khajepour, B., Marashi, R. and Parsi, T. (2013) *"Never give in and never give up": The Impact of Sanctions on Tehran's Nuclear Calculations*. National Iranian American Council (NIAC), Washington.

Newsom, N. (2014) "Iran's narratives of independence and nuclear development," *Fair Observer*, November 21. Available: http://www.fairobserver.com/region/middle_east_north_africa/irans-narratives-of-independence-and-nuclear-development-12813/ [January 7, 2017]

Portela, C. (2010) *European Union Sanctions and Foreign Policy*, New York: Routledge.

Russian International Affairs Council, RIAC (2014) *Modern Russian-Iranian Relations: Challenges and Opportunities*, Working Paper No. XIV. Moscow.

Sadjadpour, K. (2008) *Reading Khamenei: The World View of Iran's Most Powerful Leader*, Carnegie Endowment for International Peace, March 10.

Schelling, T. (1966) *Arms and Influence*, New Haven: Yale University Press.

Treaty on the Non-Proliferation of Nuclear Weapons (NPT) (1968), Article IV. Available: http://www.un.org/en/conf/2005/npttreaty.html [July 20, 2016]

van England, C. (1993) "Iran defends its pursuit of nuclear technology," *The Christian Science Monitor*, February 18. Available: www.csmonitor.com/1993/0218/18071.html [January 7, 2017]

6   The Militarization of Non-Proliferation

The most coercive instrument in proliferation is the threat of a military strike and, in the ultimate case, of a military intervention. Military threats have been an integral part of the Iran negotiation process since 2003. As the saying goes, the military option has been on the table. Israel and the US have made clear that they are more or less willing to attack Iranian nuclear facilities and destroy them by force, if need be. The EU as a civilian actor has not participated in the calls for military action. The EU's goal has been to prevent the Iraq military intervention from being repeated in Iran.

This chapter explores military threats and intervention as a tool in non-proliferation in general and in Iran in particular. In order to understand the role of the military option in the Iran case, I have looked at cases in the Middle East where military action has been used. Is there a real willingness to strike and, if so, has the use of force been effective in blocking a state's path to a nuclear weapon? Have multilateral negotiations been going on at the same time, and if so, why was the military path chosen? What were the factors preventing the use of force in the Iran case?

Nuclear Imbalance in the Middle East

There is only one country with nuclear weapons in the Middle East. Israel has possessed nuclear weapons since the 1960s and today has around 80 nuclear bombs (SIPRI, 2015). Israel developed nuclear weapons in secrecy assisted by France. Its nuclear policy is one of deliberate ambiguity or "opaque" as Israel has never admitted to having nuclear weapons. Nevertheless, it has not been willing to join the NPT as a non-nuclear-weapon state. Israel's nuclear weapons have created two very different policy options, one of a nuclear balance, the other a non-nuclear balance.

If both Iran and Israel had nuclear weapons, deterrence of a type similar to the one that existed during the Cold War would be created, resulting in stability in the Middle East, argues Kenneth Waltz (2012), a well-known scholar of international relations. According to him "power begs to be balanced," and it is surprising that in the Israeli case, it has taken so long for a balancer to emerge. He provides a radically alternative perspective on the Iran nuclear issue: "The current tensions are best viewed not as the early stages of a relatively recent Iranian nuclear crisis but rather as the final stages of a decades-long Middle East nuclear crisis that will end only when a balance of military power is restored."

A nuclear-armed Iran would, according to him, probably be the best possible result and one likely to restore stability in the Middle East. Waltz (2012:2) dismisses the whole debate on the Iranian nuclear weapon as an existential threat as language that is typical of great powers:

> which have historically gotten riled up whenever another country has begun to develop nuclear weapons of its own. Yet so far, every time another country has managed to shoulder its way into the nuclear club, the other members have always changed tack and decided to live with it. In fact, by reducing imbalances in military power, new nuclear states generally produce more regional and international stability, not less. (Waltz, 2012:2)

The opposite balance, a nuclear-weapon-free Middle East, has been on the UN and NPT agenda for decades. Already in 1974 Iran, together with Egypt, presented a resolution to the UN General Assembly on a nuclear-weapon-free zone in the Middle East. According to the resolution, states in the Middle East should adhere to the NPT as non-nuclear-weapon states and place their nuclear programs under the safeguards of the IAEA. In the voting, Israel abstained and declared that the first step should be a regional conference of states to discuss the matter. A resolution to establish a nuclear-weapon-free zone in the Middle East, later reformulated as a zone free of all WMD, has been a yearly feature in the UN General Assembly's First Committee.[1]

The extension of the NPT treaty, initially approved for only 25 years, was on the agenda of the 1995 NPT Review Conference. The Arab states, led by Egypt, opposed the indefinite extension proposed by the US, the UK and Russia, the depositary governments of the treaty. To gain Arab support for the extension, the three countries agreed to a compromise under which they would sponsor a resolution on the Middle East. The resolution called for a WMD-free zone and for all the states in the region to adhere to the NPT. The resolution was passed as part of the agreement to extend the NPT indefinitely. When the nuclear-weapon states tried to distance themselves from this at the review conference in 2000, Egypt won a reaffirmation of the resolution (Misher, 2009:3).

The 2010 NPT Review Conference agreed that the UN secretary-general and the co-sponsors of the 1995 resolution would convene a conference in 2012 on a zone free of all nuclear weapons and other WMD in the Middle East. The conference was to be attended by all states of the Middle East with the 1995 resolution as its terms of reference. In spite of intense negotiations and multilateral consultations, no conference had taken place before the NPT review conference in 2015. Due to this failure Egypt proposed that the UN secretary-general convene a conference on the Middle East zone before March 1, 2016, with countries willing to participate. The US and the UK, supported by Canada, rejected the idea, which led not only to the rejection of this resolution but also of the whole review conference. No final document could be agreed to.

Obviously, none of these nuclear balance situations are realistic today. The international community is highly unlikely to accept a situation in which Iran would acquire the bomb (and the Iranians claim that nuclear weapons are in conflict with Islam), even if it would create a "stable" balance as in the Cold War. The effort to create a nuclear-weapon-free Middle East is at an impasse.

Bombing to Avoid the Bomb

Israel's nuclear posture includes preemptive strikes as a counter-proliferation measure. This policy, known as the Begin Doctrine, is about preserving Israel's nuclear monopoly in relation to its neighbors. Prime Minister Menachem Begin explicitly stated that preemptive strikes are not an anomaly but a "precedent for every future government in Israel" (NTI, 2014). A first such strike was carried out in 1981, when Israel bombed the Osirak reactor in Iraq.

The Case of Osirak, Iraq

In 1981, Israel bombed Iraq's nuclear reactor under construction at Osirak, 17 kilometers southeast of Bagdad. On June 7, 1981, the mission was given green light as the Israel Defense Forces' chief of staff, Lieutenant General Rafael Eitan, briefed the pilots personally and told them: "The alternative is our destruction" (in Grant, 2002:75). Fourteen F-15 and F-16 fighters flew through the air space of Jordan, Saudi Arabia and Iraq and in a few minutes destroyed the French-built reactor.

Failed diplomatic efforts had preceded the attack (Yitzhak, 2003:13–14). Israeli diplomacy had engaged France and Italy, both suppliers to the reactor, and the United States. Neither the French nor the Italians wanted to cooperate. Iraq was a top customer of French military hardware, and Italy denied any involvement in Osirak. The Americans agreed that Iraq was developing a nuclear capability, a potential threat to the survival of Israel, but refused to act, possibly because Iraq was at war with Iran.

Both Italy and France maintained that the reactor was for peaceful scientific purposes. According to Israel, it was designed to make nuclear weapons. Israel claimed it had acted in self-defense and that the reactor had less than a month to go before it could no longer be attacked due to radiation fallout. Israeli Prime Minister Menachem Begin insisted that he "will not be the man in whose time there will be another holocaust." The Israeli opposition to the attack argued that the attack would unite the Arab world, be considered an act of war and harm the Israel-Egypt peace treaty (Moshe, 2003:21).

The attack was universally criticized. A UN Security Council resolution, adopted unanimously in June 1981, condemned the attack by Israel on a nuclear site approved by the IAEA and under its safeguards. The resolution further called for a cessation of hostilities, entitled Iraq to claim compensation and urged Israel to place its nuclear facilities under IAEA safeguards. As self-defense the attack was seen as a success in Israel as the reactor had "less than a month to go" before it might have been critical. Nevertheless, Iraq's nuclear program continued underground.

There are opposing views on how the strike affected the nuclear program of Saddam Hussein. US Secretary of Defense Richard Cheney in 1991 thanked the Israelis for the outstanding job they had done with the Iraqi nuclear program in 1981, which "made our job much easier in Desert Storm" (in Ivry, 2003:35). In 1997 US Secretary of Defense William Perry stated that the raid refocused the Iraqi nuclear program. Plutonium as fissile material for weapons became a lower priority, as efforts were concentrated on producing highly enriched uranium (Derfner, 2012). Iraq did continue a nuclear weapons program until it was dismantled in the aftermath of the 1991 Persian Gulf War.

The Case of Deir Ezzor, Syria

In September 2007, Israel, with the help of American intelligence, bombed an assumed nuclear facility in the Deir Ezzor region of Syria. A secret mission was launched on the night of September 6. Eight fighter planes crossed the border, undetected by Syrian air defenses, and destroyed the nuclear site. After the raid, there was a total news blackout by the Israeli and US governments. Syria denied that the facility had a military purpose. In 2011 the IAEA was able to confirm for the first time that the site was a nuclear reactor. It was assumed that Syria was planning to reprocess plutonium and produce a nuclear bomb with technical assistance from North Korea and financing from Iran (Follath and Stark, 2009).

Many details remain unclear to this day. The facility was not as near to completion as Osirak. Syria would have needed several years to reprocess the spent fuel into plutonium to make a bomb. The extent and kind of assistance provided by North Korea is unknown. None of the Arab countries nor Iran issued a protest. In the US it raised the question of the future of the six-party talks with North Korea. According to Sanger and Mazzetti (2007), the US administration did not ultimately oppose the strike. There were concerns about the ramifications of a preemptive strike in the absence of an urgent threat. Syria is a party to the NPT and was not yet obligated to declare the facility. It would have had the legal right to complete the facility as long as the purpose was to produce electricity.

Only five years after the attack did *The New Yorker* publish, under the headline "The Silent Strike," a more detailed account of what happened (Makovsky, 2012:34-40). In March 2007, Mossad, the Israeli intelligence agency, raided the Vienna home of Ibrahim Othman, the head of the Atomic Energy Commission of Syria, and obtained top-secret information from his computer. Photographs revealed a top-secret plutonium production reactor and North Korean workers on the site. The sole purpose of this kind of reactor, according to Mossad, was to produce a nuclear bomb.

In April 2007, the Bush administration asked the CIA to verify the Israeli information. The US national security advisor was to develop policy options. The facility was confirmed to be part of a nuclear program but no plutonium reprocessing plant was detected, nor was there any evidence of work on a nuclear warhead. The Israelis did not see diplomacy as a solution. In their view, it would only buy time for the Syrians, allowing them to keep working on the reactor until it was "hot" and thus make a military strike unfeasible. On the other hand, there was the risk that an Israeli raid could lead to a wider war, with both Syria and Hezbollah.

President George W. Bush finally decided, as the intelligence was "low confidence," not to lead the strike as the Israelis had wished. He told Prime Minister Ehud Olmert, "I cannot justify an attack on a sovereign nation unless my intelligence agencies stand up and say it's a weapons program" (in Makovsky, 2012:36). He proposed to send an envoy to Syria with an ultimatum to dismantle the reactor under the supervision of the five permanent members of the Security Council. The US preference for diplomacy was rejected by Olmert, who started preparations for a unilateral attack.

"The Silent Strike" compares the Syrian case with the possibility of repeating the success in Iran:

> Yet the situation in Iran differs fundamentally from the Syrian case. The Syrian affair was known to only a small number of officials in

Damascus, Israel, and Washington, whereas the prospect of striking Iran's nuclear program has been vigorously discussed in public. Experts have pointed to the risk of civilian casualties and prolonged retaliation. What's more, a key Iranian site lies deep underground outside the holy city of Qom, and it is strongly fortified; an attack on it would run a higher risk of failure. A strike might set back the Iranian program, but for how long, and at what cost? Some Israeli officials have expressed concern that a strike would only provide Iran with justification to pursue its nuclear program. (Makovsky, 2012:40)

Iraq: A Counter-Proliferation War?

At 4 p.m. on September 11, 2001, I was, as a newly appointed director, sitting in my office at COPRI, the Copenhagen Peace Research Institute. The phones started ringing; the media wanted to know what was going on. We turned on the TV, saw the planes crashing into the World Trade Center, and were just as puzzled as everyone else. What was going on? Little did we understand that it would be the start of the "war on terrorism" and the doctrine of preemptive strikes as "we have to deal with threats before they come on our shore."[2] Afghanistan was attacked, and the UN accepted this as self-defense. But at COPRI, we were amazed that just a few months later, US Secretary of Defense Donald Rumsfeld started talking about Iraq.

It did not take long before the talk was about Iraqi WMD. Iraq had had a nuclear weapons program, not known to the IAEA, until 1991, although Iraq was under safeguards. As the Gulf War ended, a UN resolution on April 3, 1991 (UNSC, 1991) established an inspection regime under which Iraq was to declare all its holdings of WMD and related facilities and programs. A special commission, UNSCOM, was created to verify Iraq's accounting of its programs to produce chemical and biological weapons programs and missiles. The IAEA would be responsible for the nuclear dimension. According to the resolution, inspections were allowed not only at declared sites, but at all sites.

The IAEA (1991) concluded that Iraq had indeed had been enriching uranium and raised questions about the peaceful nature of the program. Subsequently, Iraq declared that it had been enriching uranium with three different methods, and a document later proved conclusively that Iraq had had a nuclear weapons program (Blix, 2004:25). The program was dismantled during inspections in 1992-1998. The IAEA removed all fissionable material to Russia and supervised the destruction of installations used in the weapons programs. In a report to the Security Council in 1998, the IAEA director general declared that a "technically coherent picture" of Iraq's past nuclear program had evolved and that, although some questions remained, there were no further significant disarmament matters (Blix, 2004:28).

In July 1998, a group of international experts concluded that Iraq's biological weapons program was not verifiable. Iraq wanted to get rid of the sanctions. Consequently, Iraq's Revolutionary Command Council and the Baath Party Command decided to stop cooperation until the Security Council lifted the sanctions and reorganized the inspections. A report to the Security Council by the leader of UNSCOM in December stated that Iraq had not provided the promised cooperation. Subsequently, the US and the UK under Operation Desert Fox bombed targets in Iraq with cruise missiles. The UNSCOM mission was over. A year later, in December 1999, on the basis of reports by a UN panel, a new inspection mission, UNMOVIC, was established. Iraq was to "cooperate on all aspects" of the remaining disarmament questions in return for sanctions relief.

What followed was a race between additional inspections carried out by UNMOVIC in 2002-2003 and preparations for a military intervention in Iraq. It was also a race between the multilateral approach of the UNSC process and a unilateral action by the US (or bilateral if one includes the UK). On September 12, 2002, UN secretary-general Kofi Annan spoke at the General Assembly: "Choosing to follow or reject the multilateral path must not be a simple matter of political convenience. It has consequences far beyond the immediate context" (Annan, 2002). Furthermore, he issued a warning that preventive military action might not acquire legitimacy without the support of the UN (in Blix, 2004:73).

On February 7, 2002, Saddam Hussein had sent a letter to the Turkish prime minister stating that Iraq no longer had any WMD and had no intention of producing them. In testimony to the US Congress Robert Einhorn, former Assistant Secretary of State for Non-Proliferation, questioned whether anyone could believe Saddam Hussein. He further commented that a consensus seemed to be developing in Washington for regime change, if necessary by military force (in Blix, 2004:60). In 2002–2003 there was a clear choice between support for inspections, which would need more time, and the military option. In the Security Council there was strong opposition to a military intervention. Inspections were ongoing and Iraq finally seemed to be cooperating fully. The opposition was led by France and included Russia and Germany. The US, the UK and Spain were actively promoting the military alternative. The foreign ministers of France, the UK and Germany, who in 2003 formed the E3, were all personally present but on different sides.

In the US, the 9/11 attacks had created strong support among policy-makers for preemptive action. This is clearly reflected in the US National Security Strategy of September 2002. The strategy stated: "We must be prepared to stop rogue states and their terrorist clients before they are able to threaten or use weapons of mass destruction against the United States and our allies and friends(...)" (United States Government, 2002). Furthermore, there was widespread belief in the administration, based on intelligence information coming from defectors, that Iraq still had nuclear weapons and that inspections were an obstacle to action. Vice President Dick Cheney put forward arguments that "time is not on our side" and "risks of inaction are far greater than the risk of action" (in Blix, 2004:71).

The race ended on March 17, 2003, in the Security Council. A draft resolution by the UK in support of military action was withdrawn in the expectation that it would not pass due to a possible veto by France. Later the same day, President Bush issued an ultimatum that Saddam Hussein and his family had 48 hours to leave Iraq. Vice President Cheney said that an offer to Iraq to disarm was no longer operative. Secretary of State Colin Powell claimed that Iraq's failure to meet its disarmament obligations entitled individual members of the Security Council to take action without any collective decision by the UNSC. Operation Iraqi Freedom began early on March 20, 2003. On April 9 the government of Saddam Hussein fell. Formal combat operations ended on May 1, 2003 (Blix, 2004).

Plans to Attack Iran

In the 1990s, Israel designated Iran as a lethal threat although the two countries were geostrategic partners in the 1980s.[3] In 1987, Israeli Prime Minister Yitzhak Rabin stated at a press conference that "Iran is Israel's best friend and we do not intend to change our position in relation to Tehran" (in Makovsky, 1995:83). The mood changed in a few years and in 1993, Shimon Peres saw Iran as "insane" in its efforts to destroy Israel and urged the European states to stop flirting with Iran as the "Islamic republic is more dangerous than Hitler" (Makovsky, 1995:143). Equally, the rhetoric used later by Iran's President Mahmoud Ahmadinejad was strongly anti-Israel, denying the Holocaust and threatening the country with extinction (Gladstone, 2012).

Responding to this, Israeli Prime Minister Benjamin Netanyahu has characterized a nuclear Iran as an existential threat to Israel. The Israel chiefs of intelligence have been more cautious, asserting that an Iranian nuclear bomb would not be an existential threat to Israel. Meir Dagan, a former chief of Mossad, has argued that when presented with the option of a preemptive military strike, Israel should resort to military force only "when the knife is at its throat and begins to cut into the flesh" (Ravid, 2011). In December 2011, Dagan's successor, Tamir Pardo, addressed an audience of about 100 Israeli ambassadors. According to him Israel was using various means to foil Iran's nuclear program and would continue to do so, but if Iran actually obtained nuclear weapons, it would not mean the destruction of the state of Israel. He is quoted as saying: "Does Iran pose a threat to Israel? Absolutely. But if one said a nuclear bomb in Iranian hands was an existential threat that would mean that we would have to close up shop and go home. That's not the situation. The term existential threat is used too freely" (Ravid, 2011).

Could the successes of Osirak and Deir Ezzor be repeated in Iran? Compared to bombing Iraq and Syria, Iran was more challenging. A military attack would require a number of simultaneous attacks. Iran's nuclear facilities are more dispersed; some facilities are underground and encircled by air defenses. Furthermore, the Iranian facilities are located close to population centers. A raid would have severe consequences for civilians and most likely result in strong international criticism. Unlike the Syrian case, an Iranian nuclear program would not be stopped by a military attack.

President Bush considered the military option in 2007. The claim was, in spite of the NIE 2007, that Iran was building a bomb and arming insurgents in Iraq and Afghanistan. The administration was divided. Vice President Cheney wanted to act on Iran before the end of the Bush term. Secretary of State Rice and Secretary of Defence Gates advocated negotiations (Borger, 2007). Talks were still ongoing between HR Solana and Larijani, the Iranian chief negotiator. In 2008, during President Bush's last year in office, Israel sought bunker-busting bombs from the US in order to be able to carry out a strike on Iran. President Bush denied this request over Cheney's objections.

During President Barack Obama's first term in office, the Iranian nuclear program accelerated, as did Israel's calls for military action. A memoir of Ehud Barak, the former Israeli prime minister and leader of the labor party, reveals details of how close Israel came in 2010–2012 to striking Iran's facilities. But there was always a reason for not striking. In 2010 the IDF chief of staff said that Israel lacked operational capacity to strike. In 2011, two key ministers waffled at the last minute, and in 2012 the timing was not right because of a US-Israeli military exercise and a visit by the American defense secretary (in Rudoren, 2015).

The 2011 situation is illustrative of the cracks in Israeli-US cooperation. At the 2011 Saban Forum,[4] US Secretary of Defense Leon Panetta restated President Obama's declared position that the US had not taken any option off the table. During the question period, however, he offered a long list of reservations about the military option—for example, the difficulty of fully destroying targets and the likelihood that even a successful attack would set back the Iranian program by no more than two years. Furthermore, the Iranian regime, then approaching pariah status, would be able to mobilize renewed support at home and abroad. In addition, US interests in the Middle

East would be subject to retaliation. The economies in recession of the United States and Europe would be gravely disrupted. And worst of all, the ensuing conflagration could "consume the Middle East in a confrontation and a conflict that we would regret" (Reuters, 2011).

Just a week before the forum, General Martin Dempsey, the chairman of the US Joint Chiefs of Staff, had given a remarkably frank interview. He said that the United States was convinced that a combination of sanctions and diplomatic pressure was the right path to take on Iran, along with "the stated intent not to take any options off the table." But, he continued, "I'm not sure the Israelis share our assessment of that. And because they don't and because to them this is an existential threat ... it's fair to say that our expectations are different right now" (Reuters, 2011).

Following this, the Israel ambassador to Washington, Michael Oren, lodged an official protest with the US administration. Consequently, the Obama administration assured the Israelis that the administration had its own red lines and there was no need for Israel to act unilaterally. But the protest did lead to a reaction. In a CBS interview Panetta confirmed that all the options were on the table (CBS News, 2012).

In 2012 there was a major US study addressing the question of how the US could take the lead in carrying out a preventive military strike against Iran if all the peaceful options had been exhausted. The main conclusion was that only the US had the air power, support capability and mix of sea and air forces in the Persian Gulf to be able to sustain a campaign attacking the enrichment and research facilities, ballistic missile bases and production facilities in Iran. Israel would not have the capability to carry out a strike that could do more than delay Iran's efforts for a year or two. Furthermore, the study concludes that, while a military strike by the Israeli Air Force is possible, it would lack any assurances of a high mission success rate. As a consequence, "the U.S. expects Israel to be responsible and not to carry out such a strike" (Cordesman and Toukan, 2012: 87).

On January 23, 2012, the EU announced extensive sanctions on Iranian oil sales and the denial of Iranian access to the SWIFT financial system. These sanctions were no doubt a message to Iran to pursue negotiations, but also a message to Israel not to strike. As the chair of the European Parliament's delegation for relations with Iran I was repeatedly told that the sanctions were harsh in order to block Israel's plans to bomb Iran.

EU HR Catherine Ashton, in a joint interview on January 11, 2012 with the then-chair of the European Council, Danish Foreign Minister Villy Sövndal, underlined that "no-one was talking about military action now." She said a military conflict could be avoided and that it was time for Tehran to show willingness to negotiate. Sövndal emphasized that "[t]he reason we are so active with sanctions is precisely because they are an alternative to the military option. Everyone knows that a military attack will not solve the nuclear problem in Iran" (Politiken, 2012).

The JCPOA has not meant that the military option is no longer on the table. In a *New York Times* op-ed immediately after the deal, John Bolton, the former US ambassador to the United Nations, called for bombing Iran. Arguing that the sanctions imposed had not been crippling enough, he concluded that "[t]he inconvenient truth is that only military action like Israel's 1981 attack on Saddam Hussein's Osirak reactor in Iraq or its 2007 destruction of a Syrian reactor, designed and built by North Korea, can accomplish what is required. Time is terribly short, but a strike can still succeed" (Bolton, 2015).

What happened to the military option against Iran? This question was posed a couple of months after the JCPOA by Gary Samore, director of research at the Belfer Center for Science and International Affairs at Harvard and Ephraim Kam, a senior fellow at the Institute of National Security Studies in Tel Aviv. According to them, the military option against Iran is a problematic, complex, dangerous and controversial option. They concluded that the only two countries that would be able to carry out an attack are the US and Israel. There were, however, great differences in the two countries' attitudes towards an attack. Although the US military option has been on the table for a decade, the conditions for carrying one out have not been ripe. Israel, on the other hand, holds that it would be too late when Iran already was producing bomb-grade fissile material.

Samore and Kam (2015) underline that the military option is still on the table if Iran violates the JCPOA. But even with a violation the situation would be complicated for the US administration. What violations would justify a military attack? They conclude that the US would most likely use economic sanctions and political pressure and that even in a case of major violations, other means of pressure than the military would be used first. They assert that the American administration is most likely to carry out an attack if Iran seeks to produce weapon-grade material for a bomb.

Conclusions

The international silence that followed the Syrian bombing may be seen as tacit recognition of the inevitability of preemptive attacks on "clandestine" nuclear programs in their early stages. Nevertheless the silence raises critical questions about the respect for the internationally agreed rules of the NPT. Furthermore, bombing facilities on a foreign state's territory is also a breach of the UN Charter's Article 2, which demands that members settle their international disputes by peaceful means and refrain from the use or threat of force.

Although Israel is not a party to the NPT and consequently not bound by its rules, both Iraq and Syria were parties, and their facilities were safeguarded according to the rules of the IAEA. In the case of non-compliance the matter should have been dealt with by the IAEA and ultimately by the Security Council. Although there were international condemnations of the bombings, there were no international sanctions. It seems deeply unfair that state parties to the NPT have to follow all the rules, while states outside the NPT may bomb nuclear facilities safeguarded by the IAEA.

The Iraq war was a clear choice between a rule-based multilateral approach in the Security Council as opposed to unilateral action without a Security Council mandate. Inspections supported by the Council that would have required a few more months to conclude were terminated. The whole inspection regime was questioned and the trust in it eroded. In order to press the case for war the US administration had to "diminish, defile and dismiss inspection efforts" (Cirincione, 2003). The war not only defiled inspections, it undermined the whole nuclear non-proliferation regime.

The Iraq war was also a strong remainder of the trustworthiness the use of intelligence information in non-proliferation, particularly when it comes from an opposition source outside the country. There was, after the intervention, broad agreement that the failure to find WMD was a major blow to the credibility of US intelligence and would hamper US efforts both to "thwart nuclear smuggling and to gain support for non-proliferation steps in the United Nations" (Carus et al., 2004). President Bush's hesitancy to participate in the attack on Deir Ezzor bears witness to this as does President Obama's unwillingness to participate in a Israeli military strike on Iran in 2011-2012.

The most strategic consequence of the Iraq war was, however, the new link between non-proliferation and regime change. President Bush stated in his State of the Union address in 2003: "The gravest danger facing America and the world is outlaw regimes that seek and possess nuclear, chemical and biological weapons" (Bush, 2003). It was no longer a question of eliminating the weapons; the outlaw regimes themselves constituted the threat.

Seen from the "effective multilateralism" perspective, international norms and rules were disregarded and the legitimacy of the UN Security Council challenged. The Iraq process was a clear example of assertive multilateralism. The Security Council could be used to legitimize the war and support US interests. A resolution in favor of military intervention was withdrawn as it was not going to pass. The military intervention was initiated just a few days later. In addition to illustrating a destructive way to use the UN, the process exposed a divide among the Europeans. France and Germany fought for a multilateral approach while the UK and Spain supported military action, even without a UN mandate.

In my assessment the ongoing negotiations with Iran were a major factor in preventing a military strike. The international community would condemn such a strike, especially since the IAEA had not found that fissile material had been diverted to a military program. At the height of the threat of Israeli military intervention in 2010-2012, the EU and US unilateral sanctions were approved and expected to "cripple" the Iranian economy. It would be unacceptable to strike before the effects of these sanctions were visible.

European diplomacy seems to have had an effect also on US policies. Although the military option is still on the table, it is to be used with greater care in the case of noncompliance with the JCPOA, in fact, only if Iran is actually producing bomb-grade material.

Notes

1 The criteria for and the content of agreements on the NWFZ are described in United Nations Office for Disarmament Affairs: Nuclear-Weapon-Free Zones. www.un.org/disarmament/WMD/Nuclear/NWFZ.shtml
2 Bush statement half a year after the war (in Blix, 2004:230).
3 This was in accordance with Israel's policy of peripheral alliances (see Parsi, 2007).
4 The Saban Forum is an annual dialogue between American and Israeli leaders from across the political and social spectrum. It is organized by the Center for Middle East Policy at the Brookings Institution.

References

Annan, K. (2002) *Opening Statement to the UN General Assembly*, New York, 12 September 2002. Available: www.un.org/webcast/ga/57/statements/sgE.htm [July 16, 2016]

Blix, H. (2004) *Disarming Iraq: The Search for Weapons of Mass Destruction*, London: Bloomsbury Publishing.

Bolton, J. R. (2015) "To stop Iran's bomb, bomb Iran," *International New York Times*, November 24. Available: www.nytimes.com/2015/11/25/opinion/john-bolton-to-defeat-isis-create-a-sunni-state.html [July 16, 2016]

Borger, J. (2007) 'Cheney pushes Bush to act on Iran', *Guardian, July 16*.

Bush, G. (2003) "The 2003 State of the Union Address," Complete Transcript of President Bush's Speech to Congress and the Nation, The White House, January 28. Available: http://whitehouse.georgewbush.org/news/2003/012803-SOTU.asp [July 17, 2016]

Carus, W. S. Eberstadt, N., Einhorn, R. J., Eisenstadt, M. (2004) *The Iraq War's Impact on Nonproliferation*, Roundtable Discussion moderated by the Wisconsin Project on Nuclear Arms Control, April 14. Available: www.iranwatch.org/our-publications/roundtable/iraq-wars-impact-nonproliferation [July 17, 2016]

CBS News (2011) "Growing concern Israel may strike Iran this spring," *CBS News*, February 3. Available: www.cbsnews.com/news/growing-concern-israel-may-strike-iran-this-spring/ [July 16, 2016]

Cirincione, J. (2003) "How will the Iraq war change global nonproliferation strategies? *Arms Control Today*, April 1. Available: www.armscontrol.org/print/1238 [July 17, 2016]

Cordesman, A. and Toukan, A. (2012) *Analyzing the Impact of Preventive Strikes Against Iran's Nuclear Facilities*, Washington: Center for International and Strategic Studies, September 10. Available: http://csis.org/files/publication/120906_Iran_US_Preventive_Strikes.pdf [July 16, 2016]

Derfner, L. (2012) "The myth of the Osirak bombing and the march to Iran," *+972 Magazine*, March 2 [Online], Available: http://972mag.com/the-myth-of-the-osirak-bombing-and-the-march-to-iran/36911/

Follath, E. and Stark, H. (2009). "The story of 'Operation Orchard': how Israel destroyed Syria's Al Kibar nuclear reactor," *Spiegel Online International*, November 2 [Online], Available: www.spiegel.de/international/world/the-story-of-operation-orchard-how-israel-destroyed-syria-s-al-kibar-nuclear-reactor-a-658663.html [July 16, 2016]

Gladstone, R. (2012) "Iran's president calls Israel 'an insult to humankind,'" *International New York Times*, August 17. Available: www.nytimes.com/2012/08/18/world/middleeast/in-iran-ahmadinejad-calls-israel-insult-to-humankind.html?_r=0 [October 4, 2016]

Grant, R. (2002) "Osirak and beyond. Keeping Saddam away from mass-destruction weapons requires patience, perseverance, and an occasional bullet between the eyes," *Air Force Magazine*, August, pp. 74–78. Available: www.airforcemag.com/MagazineArchive/Documents/2002/August%202002/0802osirik.pdf [July 16, 2016]

IAEA (1991) *Statement of Director General Hans Blix to IAEA Board of Governors on 17 July 1991.*

Ivry, D. (2003) "The attack on the Osiraq nuclear reactor – looking back 21 years later," in *Israel's Strike Against the Iraqi Nuclear Reactor 7 June, 1981.* A Collection of Articles and Lecture. Jerusalem: Menachem Begin Heritage Center, p. 35.

Makovsky, D. (1995, December). *Making Peace with the PLO: The Rabin Government's Road to the Oslo Accord*, Westview Press: Boulder. Available: www.washingtoninstitute.org/uploads/Documents/pubs/MakingPeacewiththePLO.pdf.pdf [July 16, 2016]

Makovsky, D. (2012) "The Silent Strike. How Israel bombed a Syrian nuclear installation and kept it secret," *The New Yorker*, September 17, pp. 34–40.

Misher, K. (2009) *Egyptian Nuclear Leadership – Time to Realign?* Policy Outlook, 51. DC: Carnegie Endowment for International Peace. Available: http://carnegieendowment.org/files/egypt_nuclear_leadership.pdf [July 16, 2016]

Moshe, N. (2003) "Leadership and daring in the destruction of the Israeli reactor," in *Israel's Strike Against the Iraqi Nuclear Reactor 7 June, 1981*, A Collection of Articles and Lectures. Jerusalem: Menachem Begin Heritage Center, p. 21.

Nuclear Threat Initiative (NTI) (2014) *Country Profiles Israel* [Online]. Available: www.nti.org/learn/countries/israel/ [July 16, 2016]

Parsi, T. (2007) *Treacherous Alliance: The Secret Dealings of Iran, Israel, and the U.S.*, New Haven: Yale University Press.

Politiken (2012) "Ashton – no talk now of Iran military action," *Politiken*, News in English, January 11. Available: http://politiken.dk/newsinenglish/ECE1504639/ashton--no-talk-now-of-iran-military-action/ [January 16, 2016]

Ravid, B. (2011) "Mossad chief: nuclear Iran not necessarily existential threat to Israel', *Haaretz*, December 29. Available: www.haaretz.com/mossad-chief-nuclear-iran-not-necessarily-existential-threat-to-israel-1.404227 [July 16, 2016]

Reuters (2011) "Analysis: U.S. ramps up warnings on Iran strike risks," *Reuters*, December 5. Available: www.reuters.com/article/us-iran-us-idUSTRE7B427I20111205 [July 16, 2016]

Rudoren, J. (2015) "Israel came close to attacking Iran, ex-defense minister says," *International New York Times*, August 21. Available: www.nytimes.com/2015/08/22/world/middleeast/israel-came-close-to-attacking-iran-ex-defense-minister-says.html?_r=0 [July 16, 2016]

Samore, G. and Kam, E. (2015) *What Happened to the Military Option Against Iran?* Cambridge: Belfer Center for Science and International Affairs [Online] Available: http://iranmatters.belfercenter.org/blog/what-happened-military-option-against-Iran [July 17, 2016]

Sanger, D. E. and Mazzetti, M. (2007) "Israel struck Syrian nuclear project," *The New York Times*, October 14 [Online], Available: www.nytimes.com/2007/10/14/washington/14weapons.html?_r=0 [July 16, 2016]

Stockholm International Peace Research Institute (SIPRI) (2015) *SIPRI Yearbook 2015*, Oxford: Oxford University Press. Available: www.sipri.org/yearbook/2015/11 [July 16, 2016]

United Nations Security Council (UNSC) (1991) Resolution 687 (8 April 1991, S/RES/687/1991). Available: www.un.org/Depts/unmovic/documents/687.pdf [16 July 2016]

United States Government (2002) *The National Security Strategy of the United States of America*, Washington: White House. Available: www.state.gov/documents/organization/63562.pdf [July 17, 2016]

Waltz, K. (2012) "Why Iran should get the bomb: nuclear balancing would mean stability," *Foreign Affairs*, July 1, pp. 2–5.

Yitzhak, S. (2003) "The failure of diplomacy," in *Israel's Strike Against the Iraqi Nuclear Reactor 7 June, 1981*, A Collection of Articles and Lectures. Jerusalem: Menachem Begin Heritage Center, pp. 13–14.

7   Transforming the Nuclear Order
Policy Lessons Learned

In his book *The Second Nuclear Age*, Paul Bracken (2012) claims that the challenge of the second nuclear age is to manage an international order where rivalries increasingly take place in a nuclear context. The bipolarity of the first nuclear age will be replaced by multiple decision-making centers. Nuclear rivalry increasingly takes place among countries in the same region. Nuclear weapons help define a country as a major power. The number of nuclear warheads matters less.

The concepts of deterrence and arms control are, according to him, outdated and belong to the first nuclear age. The taboo of using nuclear weapons is broken as nuclear weapons are used all the time, as a political tool and as a great power symbol. Bracken sees the NPT as fiction on two accounts. Firstly, the five nuclear powers will never give up their weapons. Secondly, the nuclear-armed states outside the treaty will never sign in as non-nuclear-weapon states. Who would take North Korea seriously if it did not have nuclear weapons? Why would India renounce nuclear weapons, as it is already a de facto nuclear power?

Bracken's new multipolar nuclear system has to be controlled. Nuclear non-proliferation becomes a management problem, a problem of how to manage ambiguity and de facto double standards. Some countries are more dangerous than others. The international community could adjust to Brazil and Japan having the bomb, but not to Saudi Arabia and Algeria doing so. Treating all countries the same is democratic but not smart, he claims. The major nuclear powers, under the leadership of the US, will decide who is dangerous and who is not. New coalitions will be formed. Unless the major powers cooperate, it will be impossible to isolate and sanction a country like Iran (Bracken, 2012).

Bracken's vision is close to a worst-case scenario in terms of effective multilateralism. It implies double standards instead of a rule-based system, where states are treated equally. The major nuclear powers, under US leadership, are the global police deciding which countries are dangerous and how to control them. Many of the ingredients of his vision are present in the Iran case: double standards and ambiguity, differential treatment, isolation. Consequently, the Iran nuclear program also poses some of the critical questions for the future management of the non-proliferation regime. How can double standards be, if not eliminated, at least reduced? Can ambiguity be managed in a fair way? Will the nuclear weapon states control the nuclear order also in the future?

This final chapter offers preliminary answers to these questions. The book's two strings, the nuclear non-proliferation regime and the EU as a non-proliferation actor, are here brought together in lessons learned from the Iran case. The policy conclusions relate firstly to the management of non-proliferation: the need for a rule-based system, effective negotiations and negotiators who have faced similar problems as the target country. Secondly, the EU experience in coordinating the Iran negotiations is summarized to provide a platform for the EU's future role in non-proliferation. The chapter ends with concrete challenges to the EU as a non-proliferation actor.

Managing Non-Proliferation

The nuclear non-proliferation regime, particularly the NPT, has been muddling through for almost five decades. To continue to muddle through is not the best, nor the only option. The Iran case shows that double standards and intentional ambiguity undermine the regime. Furthermore, the NPT is not challenged only by the lack of clear rules but also by contested multilateralism. At the time of this writing there are negotiations ongoing in the UN Open-Ended Working Group about the possibility of a treaty banning nuclear weapons. Although the following lessons learned from the Iran case only relate to non-proliferation, they are also relevant for the Grand Bargain of the NPT and thus challenge the balance between the pillars.

The Need for a Rule-Based System

Nearly five years after President Bush introduced the concept of an "axis of evil" comprising Iraq, Iran and North Korea, the administration has reached a crisis point with each nation: North Korea has claimed it conducted its first nuclear test, Iran refuses to halt its uranium-enrichment program, and Iraq appears to be tipping into a civil war 3½ years after the U.S.-led invasion. (Kessler and Baker, 2006)

Today, ten years later, no WMD were found in Iraq and the country is in a civil war. North Korea, having carried out its fifth nuclear test, is a de facto nuclear-armed state. Iran has agreed to a diplomatic deal, and its paths to nuclear weapons have been blocked for the next 10–15 years.

Designating certain countries as "dangerous" is dangerous. It creates resistance and is counterproductive, if the goal is to renounce any military intentions. The "axis of evil" speech helped the hardliners in Iran, rather than the reformists.[1] It weakened the reformist president's efforts to integrate Iran into the international community. Instead of surrender, Iran built up its bargaining power. Dividing countries into those that are dangerous and those that are not, separating the "good" from the "bad," is not democratic and is not even smart, as claimed by Bracken. Using a different set of rules on each side of the divide promotes double standards and erodes the credibility of the regime. Why was Iran reported to the Security Council but not South Korea?

Which countries are treated differently today? According to an evaluation of the first ten years of the EU WMD strategy, liberal democracies are treated more leniently than others (Anthony and Grip, 2013:6). The Iran case further shows that allies, liberal or not, are treated differently. That is why South Korea was not reported. But Allies are not allies forever. The Americans supported, in spite of some warnings, the large-scale nuclear energy program of the shah. No one questioned then why a country with large oil and gas reserves would need nuclear energy. Iranian nuclear scientists were educated at MIT. The Americans were even going to sell a plutonium reprocessing plant to Iran. Kissinger, when asked about this in 2005, stated: "They were an allied country, and this was a commercial transaction. We didn't address the question of them one day moving toward nuclear weapons" (in Linzer, 2005).

The legitimacy of a number of the decisions related to the Iran case have been questioned. The war in Lebanon was not seen as a threat to world peace. How could the pilot-scale enrichment program of Iran present a threat to world peace (Kofi Annan)? Also, the six former EU Ambassadors to Tehran questioned in 2011 the justification of reporting Iran as a threat to world peace, while none of the other states enriching uranium are bothered. When is an alleged "threat to world peace" an actual threat to world peace and not only a politically defined one?

The intentional ambiguity of the rules leads to politicization of institutions such as the IAEA and the Security Council. Of course, nuclear weapons are about politics and both the IAEA Board of Governors and the Security Council are political bodies. Nevertheless, in order for the nonproliferation regime to be credible, the same rules have to apply to all. This is the essence of the EU's vision of effective multilateralism.

The intentional ambiguity of the regime is not exploited only by the veto-wielding powers of the Security Council but also by states aspiring to become nuclear weapon states. In the words of Pierre Goldschmidt:

> Today's nuclear nonproliferation regime is increasingly challenged by states that exploit ambiguity in the rules and rifts in the international community to pursue nuclear weapon capabilities without fear of reprisal. At present, lax and inconsistent compliance practices threaten nonproliferation efforts by giving some states more leeway for evading rules than should be tolerable in an effective nonproliferation regime. (Goldschmidt, 2009:1)

Clearer rules, particularly on the most sensitive part of the fuel cycle, enrichment, would benefit all. Rule enforcement, a critical demand of effective multilateralism, is not possible when major actors like the US and the EU disagree on whether or not there is a right to enrich. Nor is rule enforcement possible within a regime, where by staying outside the NPT you can avoid all the rules. An outsider state can even bomb safeguarded facilities in another state, and the only consequence is silence.

While case-by-case judgments were inevitable in the 70s, a 50-year-old treaty like the NPT should be able to overcome its initial defects. Reducing the intentional ambiguity of the treaty would not only strengthen the treaty itself, it would also make the world a safer place.

Preconditions and Regime Change

The Iran negotiations took 12 years. Given the final deal, two policies that later were abandoned prolonged the negotiations unnecessarily. The first is suspension of enrichment as a precondition for negotiations. The second is the policy of regime change. As the interest in nuclear energy increases and more states have access to nuclear technology and knowledge, the risk of proliferation grows. To carry out 12-year negotiations each time there are suspicions and allegations would hardly be appropriate and not in line with effective multilateralism. Shortcuts are not only necessary but also possible.

Firstly, a preconditions policy, requiring the suspension of enrichment before the negotiations, prevents negotiations. The EU and US agreed on the end result, zero enrichment. The difference was about suspension as a precondition for negotiations. In 2003–2005 the Europeans did achieve temporary suspension and Iran did accept the Additional Protocol. The E3 negotiated without preconditions. When the US joined in 2005, zero enrichment became a precondition. Seen from the European side, this redline was legitimate. Both the IAEA Board of Governors and the UNSC had demanded suspension. Seen from the Iranian side, the situation was different. The Iranians would have to suspend something they considered their legitimate right. The negotiations were, after the US joined in 2005, at a stalemate until the Obama administration in 2009.

With President Obama the policy changed. Zero enrichment as a precondition was abolished and more dynamic negotiations could start leading to the agreement. The Iran case demonstrates the obvious. Acceptance of a precondition—like the suspension of enrichment—before negotiations would have been a sign of weakness. To give up your core interest without getting anything in return except negotiations with an uncertain outcome was not an alternative for the Iranians. Had President Obama not abolished the precondition, frustrated, in reality frozen, negotiations might still be ongoing.

Secondly, regime change as a goal is not compatible with non-proliferation. Using a nuclear program with a suspected military dimension as a pretext for regime change marginalizes the goal of non-proliferation. A regime will not, at least not as a rule, negotiate its own exit. A regime change policy, in the Iran case, led to a situation where serious proposals from the target country were ignored. President Bush did not answer the comprehensive proposal from the reformist president Khatami in 2004 dealing not only with the nuclear issue but also terrorism, stability in the Middle East and the Israel-Palestine peace process.

How does one distinguish between non-proliferation and regime change policies? The US National Security Strategy of the same year states that the US must be able to stop "rogue states" before they are able to threaten or use weapons of mass destruction (United States Government, 2002:14). This was followed by President Bush's State of the Union Address in 2003, where he stated that the outlaw regimes seeking WMD were the gravest danger for the US (Bush, 2003). In 2003 the Bush policy of regime change not only in relation to Iraq but also in relation to Iran was clearly visible.[2]

When President Obama reached out to the Iranians, they doubted his intentions, and did not even answer. Later, by abolishing the precondition and indicating that a small pilot-scale enrichment program might be acceptable, Obama, through the Sultan of Oman, could already in 2011 convince the Supreme Leader that regime change was no longer on the table.

The Negotiators Matter

The P5+1, the five permanent members of the Security Council plus Germany, emerged as the obvious negotiating team right before the Iran case was reported to the Security Council in 2006. This formation was an ad hoc solution, supported by the council although without a formal mandate. This was possible because there was no existing entity that had a mandate.

The NPT does not have a negotiating body and the IAEA has no mandate to negotiate. The Board of Governors only judges compliance with the NPT.

Given that the Security Council would in the following years be the central actor in issuing demands on Iran, the active participation of the five permanent members was a clear asset. A veto could be avoided and compromises could be designed beforehand. When resolutions were introduced, the P5 were already on board. The unanimity of the council during the process, in spite of different interests, was remarkable.

Nevertheless, having the five nuclear-weapon states at the negotiating table is not self-evident in rule-based multilateralism for several reasons, firstly, because all these states argue that nuclear weapons are essential for their own security. Modernizing their nuclear arsenals is under way. Are these states credible actors to negotiate nuclear-free security and deterrence for others? Iran is geopolitically surrounded by more nuclear states than many other countries. Secondly, the nuclear weapon states are considered—by many of the non-nuclear weapon states—to be in breach with their Article VI obligations to disarm. Although this position is not universally accepted, it is the view of enough states to be relevant. The consequence is non-compliance with the NPT itself, not only with the reporting rules of the safeguards agreement as in the Iran case. Should countries breaking the rules negotiate the breaches of others?

There is a huge power imbalance between the nuclear and non-nuclear weapon states. The P5 control the Security Council, the ultimate judge of conflicts in non-proliferation. A country has no right of appeal and there is no arbitration mechanism if reported to the Security Council. Furthermore, the P5 also control the NPT. There is an amendment process defined in Article VIII (Treaty on the Non-Proliferation of Nuclear Weapons (NPT), 1968). Any amendment to the NPT has to be accepted by all five nuclear weapon states, giving them in effect a veto right to any changes. To guard the legitimacy of the regime, should countries without nuclear weapons not be more eligible to lead non-proliferation negotiations than countries whose nuclear weapons are undergoing modernization and protected by the NPT?

The Turkey-Brazil negotiation in 2010 shows some of the potential benefits. Two friendly, non-nuclear states negotiated a parallel agreement to the Obama "swap" deal. The former was approved by Iran, the latter rejected. Granted, there were some differences: the Turkey-Brazil declaration explicitly stated Iran's right to enrich and the LEU, while deposited in Turkey, would be under Iran's jurisdiction. However, the Obama deal was also an implicit acceptance of enrichment. The comment made by the Brazilian negotiator is illustrative: "When Brazil looks at Iran, it not only sees Iran, but also Brazil." The point is that negotiators matter and that by a strategic selection more trust can be created from the start.

Given these arguments, which countries would qualify as negotiators? Nuclear "exit" countries, meaning countries that previously possessed nuclear weapons, such as South Africa or Kazakhstan, are obvious choices. They understand the security and other consequences of a decision to abolish any intention to weaponize. Nuclear threshold states, such as Brazil or Japan, are another possibility. They know how to manage the borderline between peaceful and military uses and are under IAEA safeguards.

The critical question here is: Could the Security Council mandate a group of non-nuclear weapon states, either on an ad hoc or on a more permanent basis, to manage non-proliferation negotiations. The Security Council would decide on the mandate agreed also by the P5. The benefit would be easier and shorter negotiations resulting in less controversial agreements. Given the Turkey-Brazil experience in the Iran case, this should at least be tested.

The EU as a Global Non-Proliferation Actor

There would today be no deal without the EU. The US was deep in the morass of Iraq, damaging the transatlantic relations. This lead to the E3 initiative. Washington was opposed to these negotiations, but had no way to block them. Most were against the EU initiative, some hoped they would be successful. The EU was successful in 2003–2005. The EU protected Iran in the IAEA, blocked it being sent to the Security Council in the Board of Governors together with Russia and China. The US could not force a vote.[3]

The Collapse of the Military Option

The EU's main goal in initiating negotiations with Iran was to create an alternative to the US military intervention in Iraq. Effective multilateralism instead of unilateral military action was the strategic objective of the EU Security Strategy of 2003. This was in line with the EU's understanding of itself as a foreign policy actor—a civilian soft power promoting respect for international rules and norms. This was also what united the three EU powers in the need to talk to Iran. In 2006, the US joined into the negotiations, as did Russia and China, before Iran was reported to the Security Council in 2006. Given this coalition, the military option, while on the table all the time, was sidelined. Countries that talk do not bomb. During the 12 years of talks, there were a few critical moments. The first one was in the Security Council in 2006. The Security Council resolutions on Iran were based on Chapter VII and Iran being seen as a threat to world peace. The

Iranians expected Russia and China to veto the first resolution. This did not happen, but the two countries did oppose the reference of Iran as a threat to world peace. Both feared that this would be seen as a mandate for military action and underlined that this was not the case.

The second occasion was at the approval of the EU unilateral sanctions on Iran in 2010–2012. These sanctions were approved under US pressure and coordinated with them. The EU was initially divided on this question, both on the principle level doubting that sanctions would work and on the level of interests, as especially the Southern European states were buying Iranian oil. The winning argument here was to derail Israel's military action. During 2010–2012 the risk for Israel military action was at its height. A tight sanctions regime was a preventive measure. Furthermore, a military strike is highly unlikely under ongoing negotiations. The international community's condemnation would be immediate. The EU was successful in creating continuity in the negotiations even at times when they were in reality frozen.

Also the Americans seem to have moved towards a more non-military conclusion. Although the military option is still, even after the deal, on the table, it is limited to the case where Iran would actually be producing bomb-grade fissile material. The US would most likely use economic sanctions and political pressure in other cases of—even major—violations of the JCPOA (Samore and Kam, 2015), a sign of success for the European policy of "effective" multilateralism instead of unilateral military action.

Framing Negotiations: Creating Conditions

The JCPOA, in substance, is to a great extent a result of bilateral negotiations between the US and the Iranian teams supported by the Obama and Rouhani administrations. The Europeans, the Russians and the Chinese have had their input in discussions and comments but the basic elements are a result of bilateral talks. A symbol of these talks is the image of the two foreign ministers John Kerry and Javad Zarif walking together in the side streets of Geneva on January 14, 2015, a stroll that would have been unthinkable during decades of silent hostilities. But also a stroll that still raised criticism among the hard-liners in Iran and resulted in the foreign minister being summoned to the Iranian parliament (Balali, 2015).

These negotiations and the walk could not have taken place without the framework of the P5+1 provided by the EU. Could this have been possible without the early E3 negotiations in 2003–2005? My assessment is the E3 negotiations, while they did not reach a deal, created the necessary credibility for a diplomatic solution and in doing so sidelined the military option. The continuity of the framework created conditions for Obama to renounce the preconditions and zero-enrichment policy and for the Supreme Leader to accept the Obama proposal to negotiate. Futhermore, the P5+1 participation was a guarantee that the deal would also be approved by the Security Council.

Creating a stable arena for negotiations between hostile parties is not easy. The ups and downs of the process bear witness to the fact that the critical dimension is continuity. Although the negotiations were moved to the Security Council, where the EU does not have a seat, the P5+1 was the place for discussing the proposals presented to Iran in 2006–2013. Even when the negotiations were frozen, the framework was there and guaranteed that dates for new meetings were agreed to and meetings carried out even if no concrete results were achieved.

The importance of the framework has not been confined to providing continuity and a meeting place. Conditions for the acceptance of the final deal were also created by this arena. Both the US and Iran have been able to refer to a larger than bilateral framework when faced with domestic opposition in the approval process. The Obama administration has referred to its partners when debating the deal in Congress. The deal was the best achievable. Additional sanctions were not an alternative. Should the deal be opened, the partners of the P5+1 would withdraw their support. Along the same lines, the Iranian parliament was critical that Iran had negotiated with the US. The former head negotiator Saeed Jalili underlined during the hearing that the negotiations were not carried out with the US but with the P5+1.

The success of the EU-led framework is confirmed in the JCPOA. The Joint Commission that will monitor the implementation of the deal in the coming 10–15 years will be chaired by the EU, an international acknowledgement that the EU, and here especially the HR, has created trust as a coordinator of the P5+1.

The EU: A Unified Actor?

"Effective multilateralism" of the EU security strategy was a concept for external policies, to impact countries outside its borders. As indicated by Kienzle (2008), to see the concept only as a result of external factors, as a reaction to the Iraq war, is too limited. The concept had its deeper foundation in the EU's internal structures. There were problems with the coherence of the member states' foreign policies and with the legitimacy of the EU's own foreign policy. An umbrella concept might bridge these divides.

The fact that the E3, after disagreeing on Iraq, came together in the Iran case was an achievement, but more unintentional than one might think. The

French originally intended that the talks with Iran would take place with Russia and Germany, as all three had fought together in the Security Council against the Iraq war. The reasons for excluding the Russians and for taking the British on board instead were twofold. Firstly, the Russians would not agree to stopping enrichment. They would only go along with suspension. The British would agree to a stop. Having the Russians on board would have no bearing on the US, whereas the British would be the bridge to the US (in Davenport and Philipp, 2016).

The three major EU states negotiated in 2003–2005 as a unified front. This does not mean that there were not internal disagreements. France and the UK formed an anti-enrichment front with Germany more open to a pilot-scale enrichment program. All agreed to negotiate without preconditions and to offer Iran incentives in exchange for concessions on the nuclear program. The reporting of Iran to the Security Council had the support of all three, although there were different views on how tough the language of the resolutions should be (Bolton, 2007). Basic disagreements emerged in 2007 after the election of President Sarkozy. France became more aggressive on sanctions and saw sanctions as the only solution to the Obama "swap" deal. France even mobilized other countries for more sanctions. The situation created internal criticism. The Germans claimed that France evaded sanctions through front companies. In the bilateral phase the French opposition was even more pronounced, but did not endanger the final result. In spite of these disagreements there were no open demonstrations of major divides.

The role of the HR was critical but changed dramatically during the process: from a high representative of foreign policy to the Chair of the European council and the vice-president of the commission. This change created some friction. Firstly among the E3, who initially tried to reduce the HR role in the P5+1, and secondly with the Americans, who preferred the "facilitator" role of Solana to the "foreign minister" role of Ashton.

There were also internal conflicts between the member states. The smaller member states were initially suspicious of the big three carrying out the negotiations, particularly as the Iranian nuclear program turned out to be a very high-level and ambitious project. Frustration was related to the role of the rotating presidency not present in the negotiating team. In 2005, the year the negotiations were at the crossroads for the EU, this conflict came out in the open:

> About half a dozen member states—among them Italy, Spain and Portugal—(were) openly questioning the authority of France, Britain and Germany to negotiate a resolution at the board meeting on behalf of the European Union. (Meier, 2013:4)

A solution to the representation was found as HR Javier Solana undertook the role of a go-between and the overall EU negotiator with Iran. The EU negotiators regularly briefed the other member states in the Political and Security Committee and the Council meetings. They, however, only consulted the others if they thought that the issues would have an impact on the EU as a whole, such as with sanctions.

When the EU approved unilateral sanctions on Iran, Sweden and Finland were critical, assessing that they would not affect the Iranian nuclear program. As the sanctions would target the oil sector, Southern European countries, particularly Greece but also Spain and Italy, were initially opposed. These countries were customers of Iranian oil and, during 2012–2013, experiencing great economic difficulties due to the euro crisis. Nevertheless, the decision in January 2012 was unanimous.

As consensus was reached both on the institutional disputes as well on the sanctions, it is tempting to conclude that the EU has been a unified actor in the Iran nuclear case. Faced with an ambitious, high-level foreign policy task, the member states can bridge the divides between the big three and the rest. Also the E3 have been able to unite in face of a global problem where the EU has invested both engagement and prestige. The role of the HR has been critical in creating legitimacy for the EU's efforts and in providing common positions for the E3.

Towards Autonomy in Foreign Policy

Overall the E3/EU has acted in line with the European security strategy. Nevertheless, the EU lost its strategic capacity to act in 2005, the critical year where the EU could have acted to preserve its autonomous position and achieve a deal. There are several reasons why this did not happen. The main cause, in my view, was the split between the EU's administrative and political levels. The high-level administration saw the involvement of the Americans as critical. There would be no deal without the Americans. The political level saw US involvement as derailing the possibility of a European deal. On the other hand, in 2005 the political level of the E3 was in disarray. Dominique de Villepin became in March 2004 the Minister of Interial of France and later in March 2005 the Prime Minister. In the summer of 2005 Joschka Fisher was engaged in an election campaign and the sitting government lost the elections in September 2005. Jack Straw left as foreign minister of the UK in 2006 due to disagreements with Tony Blair on Iran. There was also the transformation refocusing the negotiations from the three member states (E3) to a more comprehensive EU approach with the HR as the coordinator. At the vital juncture, in August 2005, not only the Europeans lacked continuity. The hardliners in Iran claimed that Iran had suspended enrichment for nothing and Ahmadinejad won the presidential elections in Iran. The European autonomous position was lost.

The backbone of EU foreign policy is the transatlantic link. Also, in the new Global Strategy, a solid transatlantic partnership is seen to contribute to effective global governance. On the broader security agenda the US will continue to be the core partner (EEAS, 2016:23). The Iran negotiations tell a different story—more nuanced—about the transatlantic link.

The E3 entered negotiations with Iran in direct opposition to US unilateral action in Iraq. The policies diverged from the start. In 2005 this changed as the US pressured the EU to report Iran to the Security Council, at a time when the EU had promised Iran not to so. Even if the policies here converged, the intentions diverged. The US wanted to move the issue from the IAEA to the Security Council and keep it there. The US veto power gave it control and the possibility to pressure Iran with universal sanctions. The EU wanted to punish Iran for a while and to scare it[4] to accept a deal.

When Obama was elected president in 2009 the policies again diverged. Obama questioned zero enrichment as a precondition and let the Iranians know that some level of enrichment as the end result was possible if the conditions were otherwise right. The Europeans still maintained the zero-enrichment goal. During the "swap deal" the Europeans were split. France, in particular, saw tougher sanctions as the way forward. Other member states supported the diplomatic track. In the end the Europeans were sidelined as negotiations became bilateral. This satisfied the Americans. The only time during the process when the US saw the EU as an actual partner was in 2011–2012 as both approved unilateral sanctions.

Consequently, the Iran case provides challenging lessons in terms of the strategic autonomy of the EU's foreign policy. According to the Lisbon treaty the EU's foreign policy should not only be coherent and consistent but also autonomous:

> The EU should avoid letting its goals fall hostage to the alliances, bilateral cooperation processes, and multilateral organisations and frameworks in which it is involved. The EU should define how it stands on international issues and what its aims are for multilateral initiatives and organisations independently of what it is able to agree with its multiple partners. Agreement and consensus should be the outcome of diplomatic bargaining, not the result of self-limitation and compromises at the outset. (in de Vasconcelos, 2010:3)

The new EU global strategy is even stronger in this respect. According to HR Mogherini the ambition is strategic autonomy (EEAS, 2016:4). The Iran negotiations pose the sensitive question of how compatible, on the one hand, the goal of autonomous foreign policy based on effective multilateralism, and a rule-based global order and on the other the transatlantic link as the backbone of the EU's foreign policy, are. Are "effective multilateralism" as an EU concept and "assertive multilateralism" as the US understanding compatible in negotiations? While multilateralism for the EU is an end in itself, for the US it is a means to promote its interests. The first has respect for a rule-based order, while the second relies on a power- and interest-based order. This leads to differences on how to understand the role of international institutions, particularly of the Security Council.

The EU cannot be proud of the autonomy of its foreign policy in the Iran case. The Union will have to make clearer choices between the transatlantic link and a more autonomous foreign policy. This choice cannot be based on whoever happens to be the US president. The Iran case provides ample arguments both for cooperation with the US and for more autonomy. Nevertheless, when the US and the EU are partners, the EU is the losing party. This is clearly demonstrated by the unilateral sanctions. While their execution was coordinated and the EU took economic losses, the Americans had little sympathy for coordinating the sanctions relief in the implementation phase in a way that would satisfy European needs.

In fact, the US decisions on sanctions relief have been a great disappointment for the Europeans. Here I would like to quote my colleague in the European Parliament's Delegation for relations with Iran Marietje Schaake, today a vice president of the parliament's US delegation:

> Europe is being taken hostage by American policy. We negotiated the nuclear deal together, but now the U.S. is obstructing its execution. (in Erdbrink, 2016)

Challenges for the EU

The EU's Global Strategy, "Shared Vision, Common Action: A Stronger Europe" (2016), has a different focus from the Security Strategy of 2003. Terrorism has replaced non-proliferation of weapons of mass destruction as the major threat (EEAS, 2016:24). Non-proliferation is still on the agenda and the overall goal is:

> to widen the reach of international norms, regimes and institutions. The proliferation of weapons of mass destruction and their delivery systems remains a growing threat to Europe and the wider world. The EU will strongly support the expanding membership, universalisation, full implementation and enforcement of multilateral disarmament, non-proliferation and arms control treaties and regimes. We will use every means at our

disposal to assist in resolving proliferation crises, as we successfully did on the Iranian nuclear programme. (EEAS, 2016:41–42)

The Iranian nuclear agreement is further seen as an illustration of how agreed rules contain power politics and contribute to a peaceful, fair and prosperous world (EEAS, 2016:15). There is the need to promote reformed global governance and the "EU will promote a rule-based global order with multilateralism as its key principle and the United Nations at its core" (EEAS, 2016:8). According to the strategy this commitment translates into an aspiration to transform rather than to simply preserve an existing system.

Given this ambition of the strategy my final question is: Could the EU based on the goals of the new Global Strategy and the lessons learned from the Iran case transform the non-proliferation regime to become a more rule-based multilateral regime with the UN at its core? The elements for a transformation are there. In the Iran process the EU has built up its bargaining power and is no longer a weak actor, but a respected global actor in nuclear non-proliferation. Instead of supporting the status quo of the NPT the lessons learned in the Iran case provide a platform for a transformation. Three challenges defined below should pave the path to the needed reforms of the non-proliferation regime to a constructive future approach, rather than the current muddling through.

The First Challenge: The Implementation of the JCPOA

The successful implementation of the Iran deal will be a test case for the EU's ability to transform rather than maintaining status quo. Although the total period will be 10–15 years, the next few years will be decisive. If the Iranian people do not see the benefits of sanctions relief very soon, this will empower the opposition forces to the deal. Here the main target for the EU's persuasion will be the US administration and the Department of the Treasury. Hindrances for the ability of European banks to reengage with Iran have to be removed.

The deal's importance reaches further than the economic development of Iran in the near future. The deal has established a new negotiating mechanism between the IAEA and the Security Council, the Joint Commission. This is an arbitration mechanism to solve conflicts that may occur between the IAEA inspectors and Iran. Access to military, non-nuclear facilities and continued missile development are the already visible Achilles' heels. The use of the special procurement channel, and the potential conflicts in Iran's access to dual-use technologies, have not yet been tested.

The Joint Commission, if successful, could become a general solution to other proliferation cases and solve the NPT's lack of a negotiating facility.

This does not mean the participants would be the same, only that there is an established arbitration mechanism between the IAEA and the Security Council in each case. The structure of the Commission and its tasks and negotiating mechanisms would be designed to match each proliferation case, taking into account that "the negotiators matter."

The JCPOA also includes a third level of inspections in addtion to the comprehensive safeguards agreement and the additional protocol. The IAEA will be able to inspect undeclared sites and monitor centrifuge and component production facilities. Research will be constrained and all purchase of dual-use materials will be subject to approval. This new inspection level has already been promoted as a standard for the future. On the other hand, a number of the non-nuclear weapon states have, on the Board of the IAEA, been strongly opposed to these proposals, as they would not only undermine state sovereignity but also affect the Grand Bargain of the NPT (Cronberg, 2016). The EU as a coordinator of the Joint Commission will have a decisive role on changes in the inspection regime.

Finally, the transatlantic link has turned out to be the main challenge of the implementation phase. At the time of this writing (January, 2017) the President–elect of the US, Donald Trump is about to be inaugurated. While his administration policies on Iran and the implementation of the JCPOA are still in the dark, it is already clear that the Iran deal will be on his agenda. During the campaign he was opposed to deal, naming it a "the worst deal ever negotiated". He indicated that "dismantling the disastrous deal" would be his number 1 priority. The advisors so far elected express conflicting views on the merits of the deal. Some support it, others want to scrap it. After the election a group of Nobel laureates, veteran nuclear weapon scientists, former White House science advisers and the chief executive of the world's largest society of scientists have appealed to the President–elect to abide by the deal. (Sanger, 2017; Davenport 2016)

The EU is in a sensitive position as the chair of the Joint Commission responsible for the implementation of the JCPOA. Federica Mogherini, the HR, has already rejected, the dismantling of the deal. On November 13, 2016 she stated that it was in the European interest to guarantee that the agreement is implemented in full. Also other European leaders have underlined their commitment to the deal. (ACA, 2016) As far as the current agreeement is working, blocking effectively Iran's pathways to nuclear weapons, a collapse of the deal would be detrimental for the EU as a non-proliferation actor and support the hardliners in Iran. The first test will be the presidential elections in the spring of 2017. Seen from the European point of view the events of 2005 should not be repeated.

The Second Challenge: The Middle East Nuclear-Weapon-Free Zone

The EU´s role in non-proliferation should not be limited to, even though this is the most important part, the implementation of the Iran deal. A way to bridge the EU activities from a one state non-proliferation effort to a regional one would be to work with the Nuclear Weapon-free Zone of the Middle East. This is an issue, which has been organically linked to the permanent status of the NPT and one, which critically have been liked to the credibility of the NPT. Progress on this issue, which has burdened the NPT since 1995, would strengthen the NPT and enable future review conferences to be more successful.

Suggestions to this effect have already been made by distinguished experts in the workings of the NPT (Dhanapala, 2016:9).

The deal creates a new, if only temporary nuclear balance in the Middle East. The fear of a cascade of potential proliferation cases seems to have been avoided in the aftermath of the JCPOA (Einhorn and Nephew, 2016). The potential of a nuclear-weapon-free Middle East should be tested further in this critical situation. As a follow-up of the resolution at the 2010 Review Conference, a number of consultations were carried out, however these did not achieve the concrete result of a Middle East conference. The lack of progress on this issue was seemingly also the reason for the failure of the 2015 conference.

The EU has had a very minor role in the peace efforts in the Middle East. It has mainly softened the consequences of warfighting through humanitarian aid. The EU could gain a potential regional role and strengthen its global role by taking leadership over the further negotiations of the Middle East WMD-free zone. The platform is already there in the form of the many consultations carried out in 2012–2013. This would be a challenge where the EU could revisit its negotiation-framing experience from the Iran deal.

The Third Challenge: Strengthening Rule-Based Nuclear Multilateralism

The challenge on this issue is twofold: the ambiguity of the "inalienable" right (in Article IV) and the unspecificity of "good faith negotiation to disarm" (in Article VI). It is not easy to amend the articles of the NPT. Nevertheless, the EU, through a member state, could initiate an amendment process in relation to Article IV. The deliberate ambiguity and a case-by-case testing of the contents was no doubt appropriate when the treaty was new. Today we know more about proliferation and the conflicts in relation to the peaceful uses of nuclear technology and the related fuel cycles. A reasonable amendment reflecting the Iran process would be a clear statement on a state's right to choose its fuel cycle, including enrichment, supported by a clarification of the conditions under which this right does not apply.

In order not to modify the Grand Bargain of the treaty, this change should be accompanied by an amendment to Article VI. What is meant by initiating negotiations in good faith to achieve complete disarmament? The amendment should more clearly specify the content of the article in terms of timelines and steps to be taken. This would make the article enforceable and states could be reported to the Security Council in cases of non-compliance. Would the P5 accept this? Probably not, but if the trade-off is a treaty to ban nuclear weapons, and if non-proliferation would be strengthened by an amendment to Article IV, the conditions for an agreement might be created. In any case, to have open discussions on these necessary changes could prevent the collapse of the treaty.

The three challenges, individually and taken together, would strengthen the global role of the EU in non-proliferation and provide a central role for the Union in reforming the current nuclear order. By maintaining its goal of a rule-based international order, the EU could build the foundations for a more fair nuclear multilateralism in the face of increasing nuclear threats. The Second Nuclear Age shows one path to a new nuclear order. The EU should be able to be a leader in providing an alternative, less conflict-ridden and power-oriented path, where all states are treated equal.

Notes

1 It seems that no one had really thought about the impact. The national security advisor at the time, Condoleezza Rice, had no idea what impact the remark would have in Iran. Bush defended the wording, saying it would encourage reformers in Iran (Slavin, 2009: 200).
2 For a discussion on US policies on "rogue" and "outlier" states see Litwak (2012, 2015).
3 Author's interview with a former White House advisor on non-proliferation, Boston, May 22, 2015.
4 Author's interview with a former E3 ambassador, South England, December 18, 2015.

References

Anthony, I. and Grip, L. (2013) *Strengthening the European Union's Future Approach to WMD Non-proliferation*, SIPRI Policy Paper No. 37, Stockholm: SIPRI.
Balali, M. (2015) "Iran's foreign minister summoned to parliament over walk with Kerry," *Reuters*, January 25. Available: www.reuters.com/article/us-iran-nuclear-usa-idUSKBN0KY0MB20150125 [September 2, 2016]

Bolton, J. (2007) *Surrender an Is Not Option: Defending America at the United Nations and Abroad*. New York: Threshold Editions.

Bracken, P. (2012) *The Second Nuclear Age: Strategy, Danger, and the New Power Politics*, New York: Times Books.

Bush, G. (2003) *The 2003 State of the Union Address*, January 28, The United States Capitol, Washington. Available: http://whitehouse.georgewbush.org/news/2003/012803-SOTU.asp [September 2, 2016].

Cronberg, T. (2016) *The Great Balancing Act: EU Policy Choices during the Implementation of the Iran Deal*, EU Non-proliferation Paper No. 50, Stockholm: SIPRI.

Davenport, K. (2016) "The Iran Deal Under Trump", *Arms Control Association*, December 21. Available: https://www.armscontrol.org/print/8293 [January 7, 2017]

Davenport, K. and Philipp, E. (2016) 'A French view on the Iran deal: an interview with Ambassador Gérard Araud', Arms Control Today, July 5. Available: http://www.armscontrol.org/print/7550 [July 20, 2016]

de Vasconcelos, Á. (ed.) (2010) *A Strategy for EU Foreign Policy*, Report No. 7, June, Paris: European Union Institute for Security Studies. Available: http://www.iss.europa.eu/uploads/media/A_strategy_for_EU_foreign_policy.pdf [September 2, 2016]

Dhanapala, J. (2016) *Who Is Afraid of Consensus? The NPT Review Process*, Issue Brief, James Martin Center for Nonproliferation Studies, Monterey: Middlebury Institute for International Studies. Available: www.nonproliferation.org/wp-content/uploads/2016/08/who-is-afraid-of-consensus.pdf [September 2, 2016]

Einhorn, R. and Nephew, R. (2016) *The Iran Nuclear Deal: Prelude to Proliferation in the Middle East?* Foreign Policy at Brookings, Arms Control and Non-Proliferation Series, Paper 11, May. Available: www.brookings.edu/wp-content/uploads/2016/05/acnpi_20160531_iran_deal_regional_proliferation.pdf [September 2, 2016]

Erdbrink, T. (2016) "Europe says U.S. regulations keeping it from trade with Iran," *International New York Times*, April 21. Available: www.nytimes.com/2016/04/22/world/middleeast/europe-says-us-regulations-keeping-it-from-trade-with-iran.html [September 2, 2016]

European External Action Service (EEAS) (2003) *European Security Strategy: A Secure Europe in a Better World*, December 12, Brussels. Available: www.consilium.europa.eu/uedocs/cmsUpload/78367.pdf [September 2, 2016]

European External Action Service (EEAS) (2016) *A Global Strategy for the European Union's Foreign and Security Policy. Shared Vision, Common Action: A Stronger Europe*, June, Brussels. Available: https://eeas.europa.eu/top_stories/pdf/eugs_review_web.pdf [September 2, 2016]

Goldschmidt, P. (2009) *Concrete Steps to Improve the Nonproliferation Regime*, Carnegie Papers, Nonproliferation Program, Number 100, April, Washington: Carnegie Endowment for International Peace. Available: www.ciaonet.org/attachments/14067/uploads [July 18, 2016]

Kessler, G. and Baker, P. (2006) "Bush's 'Axis of Evil' comes back to haunt United States," *The Washington Post*, October 10. Available: www.washingtonpost.com/wp-dyn/content/article/2006/10/09/AR2006100901130.html [September 2, 2016].

Kienzle, B. (2008) *The EU and the International Regimes in the Field of Non-Proliferation of Weapons of Mass Destruction*, Conference Paper, CARNET Conference, Egmont Palace, Brussels, April 24–26.

Linzer, D. (2005) "Past arguments don't square with current Iran policy," *The Washington Post*, March 27. Available: www.washingtonpost.com/wp-dyn/articles/A3983-2005Mar26.html [September 2, 2016]

Litwak, R. (2012) *Outlier States: American Strategies to Change, Contain or Engage Regimes*, Baltimore: John Hopkings University Press.

Litwak, R. (2015) *Iran's Nuclear Chess: After the Deal*. Washington D. C.: Wilson Center Middle East Program.

Meier, O. (2013) European Efforts to Solve the Conflict over Iran's Nuclear Programme: How Has the European Union Performed?, EU Non-Proliferation Consortium: Non-Proliferation Papers, No. 27, February. Available: www.sipri.org/research/disarmament/eu-consortium/publications/nonproliferationpaper-27 [July 20, 2016]

Samore, G. and Kam, E. (2015) *What Happened to the Military Option Against Iran?* Cambridge: Belfer Center for Science and International Affairs. [Online] Available: http://iranmatters.belfercenter.org/blog/what-happened-military-option-against-Iran [July 17, 2016]

Slavin, B. (2009) Bitter Friends, Bosom Enemies: Iran, the U.S., and the Twisted Path to Confrontation. New York: St. Martin's Press.

Treaty on the Non-Proliferation of Nuclear Weapons (NPT) (1968), Article IV. Available: www.un.org/en/conf/npt/2005/npttreaty.html [July 20, 2016]

United States Government (2002) *The National Security Strategy of the United States of America*, Washington: White House. Available: www.state.gov/documents/organization/63562.pdf [September 2, 2016].

Glossary

Additional Protocol   A legal document granting the IAEA complementary authority to verify a State's safeguards obligations.

A. Q. Khan network   A Pakistani network that provides access to nuclear weapons technology.

Breakout time   The time needed to produce a bomb after a decision to do so.

Bushehr   Nuclear power plant in Iran, started in the 1975 by German companies but stopped in 1979. Russia took over the contract in 1995.

Eurodif   A subsidiary of the French company AREVA to enrich uranium. Iran was a shareholder via Sofidif, a French-Iranian enterprise.

Fissile material   Material capable of sustaining a nuclear fission chain reaction.

Fuel rods   A rod-shaped fuel element in a nuclear reactor containing uranium-oxide pellets.

Guardian Council   Reviews legislation to make sure that it conforms to Islamic law and vets election candidates in relation to Islam.

Heavy water reactor   A nuclear reactor using unenriched natural uranium as its fuel with heavy water as its coolend and neutron moderator.

Islamic Revolutionary Guard Corps (IRGC)   A military organization in Iran responsible for the protection of the revolutionary values and the survival of the regime.

Level of enrichment   The degree of uranium 235 in the material.

Majles   The 290-member parliament that of Iran directly elected by the population.

Mojahedin-e-Khalq (MEK)   Iranian opposition group working from Paris and Iraq. Formerly on the EU and US terrorist lists, now removed.

New Agenda Coalition   A group of states (Ireland, Sweden, Egypt, Mexico, Brazil, New Zealand and South Africa) established in 2000 seeking to build an international consensus to make progress on nuclear disarmament, as legally called for in the NPT.

Nuclear Suppliers Group (NSG)   A group of suppliers that define guidelines for nuclear exports and nuclear-related exports.

Nuclear-weapon-free zone (NWFZ)   A group of states, established by treaty or convention, that prohibit nuclear weapons in a given area.

Possible military dimension (PMD)   Activities of a state seen as indications of nuclear weapon intentions.

Reprocessing (spent fuel, plutonium)   A technology developed to chemically separate fissionable plutonium from irradiated nuclear fuel.

Safeguards Agreement   Rules of the IAEA to verify that a state does not to use nuclear material for weapon purposes.

Supreme Leader, The   Head of state and highest ranking political and religious authority in Iran.

Suspension of enrichment   a requirement by the IAEA/UNSC for Iran to stop enriching uranium.

"Swap" deal, The   The transformation of Iranian LEU to fuel rods for the Tehran Research Reactor in another country.

Threshold state   A state that has the capacity to produce a nuclear weapon but has not decided to do so.

Uranium conversion   Transformation of natural uranium to uranium hexafluoride gas.

Uranium enrichment   Uranium hexafluoride gas (UHF6) is fed into and concentrated in centrifuges to increase the level of U-235 isotope.

Weapons of mass destruction (WMD)   Biological, chemical and nuclear weapons.

Index

Printed and bound by CPI Group (UK) Ltd, Croydon, CR0 4YY

08/06/2025

01896991-0006